Milestones ©

Workbook

with Test Preparation

HEINLE
CENGAGE Learning™

Australia · Brazil · Japan · Korea · Mexico · Singapore · Spain · United Kingdom · United States

**Milestones C Workbook
with Test Preparation**

Editorial Director: Joe Dougherty

Publisher: Sherrise Roehr

Managing Editor: Carmela Fazzino-Farah

Associate Development Editor: Stephen Greenfield

Technology Development Editor: Debie Mirtle

Executive Marketing Manager: Jim McDonough

Director of Product Marketing: Amy T. Mabley

Product Marketing Manager: Katie Kelley

Assistant Marketing Manager: Andrea Bobotas

Director of Content and Media Production:
Michael Burggren

Production Assistant: Mark Rzeszutek

Manufacturing Manager: Marcia Locke

Development Editor: Arley Gray

Composition and Project Management:
ICC Macmillan; Valuechain International

Interior Design: Rebecca Silber

Cover Design: Page 2, LLC

Cover Image: Joseph Sohm/Visions of America/Corbis

ISBN-13: 978-1-4240-3212-9

ISBN-10: 1-4240-3212-1

Heinle
25 Thomson Place
Boston, MA 02210
USA

Cengage Learning is a leading provider of customized learning solutions with office locations around the globe, including Singapore, the United Kingdom, Australia, Mexico, Brazil, and Japan. Locate your local office at:
international.cengage.com/region

Cengage Learning products are represented in Canada by Nelson Education, Ltd.

Visit Heinle online at **elt.heinle.com**
Visit our corporate website at **cengage.com**

Printed in the United States of America
1 2 3 4 5 6 7   12 11 10 09 08 07

Contents

UNIT 4: Cultures and Traditions

UNIT 5: Making a Difference

Chapter 2

UNIT 6: Leadership

Milestones C • Copyright © Heinle

Assessment Practice

tegies for Testing Success

ood readers will develop many different reading skills. To become a good reader, you will
to learn to read different kinds of texts. Many tests measure your reading skills. You will soon
ne of these tests. The test will ask many questions, each with four possible answers. You must
e the correct one.

ere are some of the things you will be tested on:

The meanings of words
The main idea of a passage
What happens in a story
Why an author wrote a passage
Comparing two or more things
Understanding cause and effect
Using materials to find information

.ing Ready for Test Day

he following is a list of things that can help you get ready for a test.

Read at least thirty minutes per day.
Practice reading all different kinds of materials (newspapers, magazines, informational texts,
novels, stories, poetry, etc.).
Set a daily time for studying and doing your homework.
Set up a place to do your homework every day. Make sure it is quiet and well lit.
Practice answering each kind of question that will be on the test (multiple-choice,
short-response, and extended-response).
Review simple test-taking strategies.
Practice timed activities.
Get enough sleep the night before the test.
Eat a good breakfast on the day of the test.

What to Expect During a Test

The *Milestones* program will help you acquire and master the skills you will need to succee in English. It will aid your progress in the following four skills: listening, speaking, reading, a writing.

You are about to take an assessment practice test. The purpose of the test is to measure you achievement in constructing meaning from a wide variety of texts. This practice includes many different kinds of reading passages followed by specific questions about the passages.

Each reading passage will be different. Some types of passages include factual articles, fict stories, and poems. Always read the passages carefully. You can go back to a passage if you ar sure about something.

After reading each passage, you will then answer questions about the passages. Read the questions carefully. They will ask about parts of the passages such as facts, plot, or language.

On the actual test, you may also be given a map, chart, or picture. For those, you will have read the titles and labels to answer the questions.

Your teacher will give you sample directions and questions before the test begins. Ask abou anything you do not understand. Once the test begins, you will not be able to ask questions.

The test questions all have multiple-choice answers. A multiple-choice test item may ask y to answer a specific question, or it may ask you to complete a sentence. There will be four pos answers. Only one of them is correct. Read all of the choices carefully and choose the answer think is correct. Don't spend too much time on one question. It is important to answer all of th questions on the test.

How to Read Questions

ne following is a sample passage. Read the passage and then read the questions below.

ery morning, Isabella and her mother walk together to school. Isabella's mother always smiles ays, "Isabella, be careful when you cross the street." Her smile is gentle like a flower.

Read this sentence from the passage.

> Be careful when you cross the street.

What is the meaning of <u>careful</u> in this sentence?

A cautious

B bored

C happy

D tired

Which word best tells about Isabella's mother's attitude toward Isabella?

A patient

B clever

C nervous

D understanding

ou will be asked to use a number two pencil on the test. Be sure to mark the correct answer on swer sheet. Make sure the number on the answer sheet matches the number of the question. It y to make a mistake. If you do, your answers will be marked as wrong because they are in the place. Do not change an answer unless you are sure that it is wrong. If you must change an r, check the number and change the right one. Make sure that you answer every question. Do ave any answers blank.

How to Answer Questions

When answering multiple-choice questions, read each answer carefully.

3 **Read this sentence from the passage.**

> Her smile is gentle like a flower.

What literary device is demonstrated in this sentence from the passage?

A simile

B metaphor

C onomatopoeia

D personification

You might say: *I see that this question is asking about a literary device. I also see that example of literary devices are possible answers. There aren't any sounds in the sentence, so it is not onomatopoeia. There is no comparison to a person, so it is not personification. A thing is not described as another thing, so it is not metaphor. However, the word "like" is used, so it must be simile. Therefore, the correct answer is letter a. This question is number 3. I will look at my answer sheet, find number 3, and mark letter a.*

The following pages contain an assessment practice test. Read each passage carefully. Then use the answer sheet on page 5 to mark your answers.

er the questions that appear in the Assessment Practice Test on this Answer Sheet.

Ⓐ Ⓑ Ⓒ Ⓓ	27 Ⓐ Ⓑ Ⓒ Ⓓ	53 Ⓐ Ⓑ Ⓒ Ⓓ
Ⓐ Ⓑ Ⓒ Ⓓ	28 Ⓐ Ⓑ Ⓒ Ⓓ	54 Ⓐ Ⓑ Ⓒ Ⓓ
Ⓐ Ⓑ Ⓒ Ⓓ	29 Ⓐ Ⓑ Ⓒ Ⓓ	55 Ⓐ Ⓑ Ⓒ Ⓓ
Ⓐ Ⓑ Ⓒ Ⓓ	30 Ⓐ Ⓑ Ⓒ Ⓓ	56 Ⓐ Ⓑ Ⓒ Ⓓ
Ⓐ Ⓑ Ⓒ Ⓓ	31 Ⓐ Ⓑ Ⓒ Ⓓ	57 Ⓐ Ⓑ Ⓒ Ⓓ
Ⓐ Ⓑ Ⓒ Ⓓ	32 Ⓐ Ⓑ Ⓒ Ⓓ	58 Ⓐ Ⓑ Ⓒ Ⓓ
Ⓐ Ⓑ Ⓒ Ⓓ	33 Ⓐ Ⓑ Ⓒ Ⓓ	59 Ⓐ Ⓑ Ⓒ Ⓓ
Ⓐ Ⓑ Ⓒ Ⓓ	34 Ⓐ Ⓑ Ⓒ Ⓓ	60 Ⓐ Ⓑ Ⓒ Ⓓ
Ⓐ Ⓑ Ⓒ Ⓓ	35 Ⓐ Ⓑ Ⓒ Ⓓ	61 Ⓐ Ⓑ Ⓒ Ⓓ
Ⓐ Ⓑ Ⓒ Ⓓ	36 Ⓐ Ⓑ Ⓒ Ⓓ	62 Ⓐ Ⓑ Ⓒ Ⓓ
Ⓐ Ⓑ Ⓒ Ⓓ	37 Ⓐ Ⓑ Ⓒ Ⓓ	63 Ⓐ Ⓑ Ⓒ Ⓓ
Ⓐ Ⓑ Ⓒ Ⓓ	38 Ⓐ Ⓑ Ⓒ Ⓓ	64 Ⓐ Ⓑ Ⓒ Ⓓ
Ⓐ Ⓑ Ⓒ Ⓓ	39 Ⓐ Ⓑ Ⓒ Ⓓ	65 Ⓐ Ⓑ Ⓒ Ⓓ
Ⓐ Ⓑ Ⓒ Ⓓ	40 Ⓐ Ⓑ Ⓒ Ⓓ	66 Ⓐ Ⓑ Ⓒ Ⓓ
Ⓐ Ⓑ Ⓒ Ⓓ	41 Ⓐ Ⓑ Ⓒ Ⓓ	67 Ⓐ Ⓑ Ⓒ Ⓓ
Ⓐ Ⓑ Ⓒ Ⓓ	42 Ⓐ Ⓑ Ⓒ Ⓓ	68 Ⓐ Ⓑ Ⓒ Ⓓ
Ⓐ Ⓑ Ⓒ Ⓓ	43 Ⓐ Ⓑ Ⓒ Ⓓ	69 Ⓐ Ⓑ Ⓒ Ⓓ
Ⓐ Ⓑ Ⓒ Ⓓ	44 Ⓐ Ⓑ Ⓒ Ⓓ	70 Ⓐ Ⓑ Ⓒ Ⓓ
Ⓐ Ⓑ Ⓒ Ⓓ	45 Ⓐ Ⓑ Ⓒ Ⓓ	71 Ⓐ Ⓑ Ⓒ Ⓓ
Ⓐ Ⓑ Ⓒ Ⓓ	46 Ⓐ Ⓑ Ⓒ Ⓓ	
Ⓐ Ⓑ Ⓒ Ⓓ	47 Ⓐ Ⓑ Ⓒ Ⓓ	
Ⓐ Ⓑ Ⓒ Ⓓ	48 Ⓐ Ⓑ Ⓒ Ⓓ	
Ⓐ Ⓑ Ⓒ Ⓓ	49 Ⓐ Ⓑ Ⓒ Ⓓ	
Ⓐ Ⓑ Ⓒ Ⓓ	50 Ⓐ Ⓑ Ⓒ Ⓓ	
Ⓐ Ⓑ Ⓒ Ⓓ	51 Ⓐ Ⓑ Ⓒ Ⓓ	
Ⓐ Ⓑ Ⓒ Ⓓ	52 Ⓐ Ⓑ Ⓒ Ⓓ	

Ode to an Arachnid
Anonymous

While walking down a pathway,
  at a slow and steady pace,
Some threads so slight and sticky
  brushed across my frightened face.
They tangled in my hair and then   5
  they stuck to arms and chest!
I waved my arms and shouted,
  so confused and so distressed!

I brushed my face and body,
  as I took a step or two   10
Then turned around to take a look
  and see what I'd walked through.
At first I noticed nothing
  but the trees at left and right,
Then near a leafy tree-branch,   15
  something strange came into sight.

There, swinging by a tiny thread,
  just half an inch, no wider,
There was a little, tiny, fat,
  unhappy-looking spider!   20
His tiny voice demanded,
while six angry fists he shook,
"Next time you walk through nature,
  open up your eyes and look!"

I suddenly felt guilty,   25
  and a tear came to my eye,
Just thinking of the pain I'd caused
  that small eight-legged guy.
While walking down that shady path,
  my auntie Jeanne's house leaving,   30
In seconds I'd undone the web
  he'd spent the long day weaving!

Open Windows
Sara Teasdale (1884–1933)

f the window a sea of green trees
their soft boughs like the arms of a dancer;
beckon and call me, "Come out in the sun!"
I cannot answer.

alone with Weakness and Pain,   5
abed and June is going,
ot keep her, she hurries by
the silver-green of her garments blowing.

and women pass in the street
of the shining sapphire weather,   10
e know more of it than they,
and I together.

are the runners in the sun,
thless and blinded by the race,
e are watchers in the shade   15
speak with Wonder face to face.

Demeter and Persephone
An Ancient Greek Myth

Demeter was the Greek goddess of the harvest. She controlled the growing of the trees, flowers, grain
nd fruits. Her daughter was a beautiful girl named Persephone. One day, Persephone was in the field
athering flowers, when Hades, the king of the underworld, saw her and wished to marry her. He took her
ith him to his dark halls beneath the Earth.

Demeter was very sad. She asked Zeus, the king of the gods, to help. Zeus said he could bring
ersephone back only if she had not eaten anything in Hades, which was also the name of the
nderworld. However, Persephone had already eaten a pomegranate, so she could not return to Earth.
Demeter was so upset that she stopped caring about the plants and trees. The grass became brown, the
owers died, and the trees lost their leaves. Seeing this, Zeus called an emergency meeting with Demeter
nd Hades. After much discussion, they reached a compromise: for part of the year, Persephone would
emain on Earth with her mother. For the other part, she would go to the underworld as Hades's wife.

So each year, when Persephone returns to Earth, the flowers bloom, and we call it spring. Then, when
ersephone goes to Hades, her mother becomes sad, the plants turn brown, and we call it winter. And so
he cycle continues every year, from spring to autumn, autumn to spring, for all eternity.

1 What genre of writing is "Ode to an Arachnid?"

A   short story

B   poetry

C   fiction

D   drama

2 Read this sentence from "Ode to an Arachnid".

> I waved my arms and shouted, so confused and so <u>distressed</u>!

What is the meaning of <u>distressed</u> in this sentence?

A   upset

B   satisfied

C   disgusted

D   pleased

3 Why did the narrator feel guilty?

A   He tore the spider's web.

B   He stepped on the spider.

C   He left his aunt's house early.

D   He broke the branch of the tree.

4 What is the author talking about whe he or she writes "threads so slight and sticky"?

A   the spider

B   the tree branch

C   the narrator's hair

D   the spider's web

5 In the poem "Open Windows," what c the author compare the branches of a to?

A   jewels

B   arms

C   runners

D   garments

6 What does the author mean when he "June is going"?

A   Leaves are falling.

B   People are running.

C   Time is passing.

D   The sun is shining.

What is the meaning of <u>beckon</u> in the first stanza of "Open Windows"?

A   refuse to take notice of

B   form a mental image of

C   signal with a gesture

D   pay careful attention to

What is similar between "Ode to an Arachnid" and "Open Windows"?

A   Both show how people affect the world.

B   Both authors use figurative language.

C   Both reflect the anger of nature.

D   Both are about Greek gods.

What happened when Demeter was sad in "Demeter and Persephone"?

A   The skies turned cloudy and dark.

B   Persephone could not return to Earth.

C   The flowers and plants died.

D   Zeus would come to cheer her up.

10 **What does the word <u>compromise</u> mean in paragraph 2?**

A   when one person gets everything that he wants

B   a decision that is forced upon someone

C   an agreement that makes each side somewhat happy

D   a situation that gets worse as time goes on

11 **What is the problem in the story?**

A   Persephone did not want to return to Earth.

B   Zeus had no control over the king of the underworld.

C   Demeter would not agree to share her daughter.

D   Hades took Persephone to the underworld.

12 **What are all three passages about?**

A   nature

B   danger

C   weather

D   anger

My Aunt Tina

1   Julio knocked on David's door and waited. Finally, David opened the door and peeked out. Altho
it was a sunny Saturday morning, it looked dark inside.

2   "Hey, David, let's go climb Pott's Hill! We can pretend we're on a secret scout mission..."

3   "Not right now. I'm playing Street Boxer XII."

4   "Video games? But Dave, look at the weather! How can you stay inside?"

5   "Easy! I just don't go out! Anyway, I'm working on my martial arts skills."

6   "How can you work on your martial arts skills when you're just sitting there, not moving?"

7   "Hey, I move!" David demonstrated how his thumbs twitched and turned on the control pad.

8   Julio shook his head. "Listen, let me tell you a story about my aunt Tina. It's a sad story, so pay atten
When she was young, Tina was a fun girl who loved to play outside. She went for walks, climbed trees, a
played in the sun. Then her family bought a big TV, and for her birthday they gave her a video game cons
At first, she didn't know what to do with it. Then she started to get interested. She played more and more.
and eventually she only wanted her friends to visit her if they would play video games. Soon she became
obsessed, and when she lost, she got really mad. Her friends stopped coming over."

9   "Pretty soon, Tina was playing all day and watching TV all night. She never left the TV room. He
parents were worried, but they couldn't talk to her. She would only stare at the screen. They tried turn
off the TV, but Tina would scream if they touched it. She didn't want to exercise at all. She would onl
move like this." Julio imitated David's earlier thumb-moving demonstration. "Eventually, she stoppec
moving at all. She just sat and stared with her eyes wide and her mouth hanging open like this." Julio
demonstrated. He stared blankly past David. He stayed like that, without saying anything, for a long t
Finally, David pushed Julio's shoulder roughly with his right hand.

10   "Hey, I get the picture! What happened next?"

11   "Finally, her parents decided to do something. They threw the video game set out the window and
hauled away the TV. Tina just kept staring at the wall, like this." Again, Julio widened his eyes and le
mouth hang open. "Finally her parents lifted her and carried her to the front yard. They put her down,
she stayed there, staring out into the street, for three days! Finally, they took her to the hospital, and a
about five years she got better."

12   David was so startled by the story that he shut off the TV, and went outside with Julio. The two b
walked to Pott's Hill, and David breathed the fresh summer air. Suddenly, he remembered something.
"Wait," he said, "you don't even have an aunt Tina!"

13   Julio just shrugged and began to whistle.

Why doesn't David want to go outside?

A   He doesn't want to be with Julio.

B   He is working on his martial arts skills.

C   He thinks it's night because it's dark inside.

D   He is too involved playing video games.

Which word is related to <u>interested</u>?

A   obsessed (paragraph 8)

B   demonstrated (paragraph 7)

C   abandoned (paragraph 8)

D   imitated (paragraph 9)

How was the problem of the story "My Aunt Tina" resolved?

A   Julio gets David to come outside.

B   David invited Julio to play video games.

C   David met Julio's Aunt Tina.

D   Julio goes to Pott's Hill by himself.

16   **Why did friends stop coming to Tina's house?**

A   She stopped inviting them.

B   She became selfish and angry.

C   They got their own video games.

D   They wanted to spend time outside.

17   **What does the phrase "I get the picture" mean in paragraph 10?**

A   I'll do it.

B   I remember

C   I understand.

D   I'm listening.

18   **Why did Tina stay on her front yard staring into the street for three days?**

A   She was waiting for her friends.

B   She was too large to move.

C   She was hurt.

D   She was tired.

The following is a rough draft of a student's journal, which may contain errors.

My Weekend Observations

Tania Vieira

Saturday, April 5

1   Today I went to the hospital to visit my brother. Late last night, he woke up with a pain in his abdomen, and he felt really sick. He was crying a lot, and we were really worried. My father drove hi to the hospital, and the doctor said his appendix had to come out right away. They call this operation "appendectomy."

2   This was my first time inside a hospital since I was a baby. Everything seemed white and clean, t there was a strange smell in the air. It was a combination of bleach, sickness, and hospital food. Whe got to my brother's room, he looked tired and weak, so I gave him a present: It was a balloon that sai "Get Well." He smiled.

3   Suddenly, the smells of the hospital became stronger. The room started spinning, and everything went black. When I woke up, I was looking up at the ceiling, and my mother and a nurse were over n had fainted! I lying in the hospital bed next to my brother's. When my aunt arrived at the front desk tl morning, she said she wanted to visit the patient with the last name "Vieira." She was shocked when t receptionist answered, "Which one: Mario or Tania?"

The following is a rough draft of a student's report, which may contain errors.

1   *The Neverending Story* by Michael Ende is a story within a story. The main character is a lonely I named Bastian who is not popular at school. His mother has died, and his father doesn't seem interest in him. One day, Bastian enters an antique book shop, and he gets a strange, old book called *The Neverending Story*. He brings it home and begins to read about a strange world called Fantastica. Bec the book is a story within a story, it is printed in two colors: red when we are reading Bastian's story i the "real" world, and green when we are reading about Fantastica.

2   Fantastica is a world in trouble. A mysterious force called the Nothing is taking over, and the Childlike Empress who rules the land is very ill. She asks a young warrior named Atreyu to help her find the cure. As Bastian reads the story, he slowly becomes part of the story until he literally become a character in Fantastica! Bastian then saves the Empress by giving her a new name: He calls her Mo Child. Bastian goes on to have many adventures with Atreyu and a magical amulet called Auryn. Late he finishes his role in the story and returns to "real" life, where he realizes that his life has changed— that he has changed, too.

How was the setting important to the student's journal?

A   She always wanted to visit someone in the hospital.

B   It upset her that her brother needed an operation.

C   It was the smells of the hospital that made her faint.

D   She liked the balloon she gave to her brother.

What is the journal mostly about?

A   having an operation

B   a hospital visit

C   what to do if you faint

D   hospital food

Read this sentence from the student's journal.

> It was a <u>combination</u> of bleach, sickness, and hospital food.

What is the meaning of <u>combination</u> in this sentence?

A   a mixture

B   an element

C   a description

D   a portion

22   **What kind of writing is *The Neverending Story*?**

A   fantasy

B   realistic fiction

C   drama

D   poetry

23   **Who wrote the passage?**

A   the author of the book

B   the main character, Bastian

C   a character from Fantastica

D   a reader of the book

24   **What does the reader think is most important about *The Neverending Story*?**

A   Bastian visits an antique book shop.

B   It is a story within a story.

C   Bastian gets an amulet called Auryn.

D   The Childlike Empress doesn't have a name.

The following is a rough draft of a student's essay, which may contain errors.

1   Salif Keita is a popular singer from Mali, a country in Africa. His music combines traditional We
African and Islamic music styles with modern European and American elements. Some of the traditio
African instruments you can hear on his albums are: the *kora*, a gourd-like stringed instrument with a
long, thin neck; the *djembe*, a common West African drum; and the *balafon*, a percussion instrument
resembling a xylophone. Some modern instruments he uses are the guitar, the saxophone, and the
keyboard.

2   Keita was born in 1949, in Djoliba, Mali. He is a direct descendant of Sundjata Keita, a great war
and prince. Sundjata unified the Mandinka people and founded the Malian Empire in the 13th century
The Malian Empire was a large West African state that stretched from the west coast to Timbuktu, a
city in present-day Mali. It lasted from the year 1235 to 1610. The Mandinka people dominated the
region, but many other ethnic groups lived there, too. Sundjata Keita is also known as the "Lion King
Mali." This is because part of his name, Jata, means "lion," and also because he was brave and power
Malians consider him one of the great heroes of their history.

3   Because Salif is from a prestigious royal line, he deserves respect from his family and from socie
However, he is albino. This means that he lacks pigment in his skin, hair, and eyes. Because of this, h
vision is not very good. Many of the Mandinka people believe that albinos brought bad luck. So, both
family and the community rejected him.

4   As a result, Salif went to Bamako and became a musician. At first, this was hard for people to acc
Malians considered music to be the wrong path for someone of royal heritage. In their tradition, only
griots were supposed to be singers. Griots were traditional West African storytellers, the keepers of o
tradition and history in song. They formed a special class of people in society. Generally, a person wh
was not from a griot family would not become a griot. However, Salif's powerful voice was so good,
he quickly gained popularity. People overcame their prejudices about Salif's color and family origins
country embraced him as a beloved star.

5   Salif joined the band Les Ambassadeurs in 1973. He moved with the band to Ivory Coast in the
mid-70s because of political problems in Mali. There, the band became very successful and well-kno
Salif later moved to Paris to bring his unique music and culture to Europe. There, he became a huge
international star.

6   In 2004, Salif decided to return to live permanently in Mali. He opened a recording studio in
Bamako, where he recorded his album M'Bemba in 2005. In it, he returned to his musical and histori
roots. After overcoming many obstacles and achieving great success, Salif Keita could finally come b
to his home. He is now respected and revered in Mali and abroad as the "Golden Voice of Africa."

How did things change for Salif by the end of the passage?

A His family and community rejected him.

B He could only find success in Europe.

C He was welcomed home as a hero.

D He became active in the politics of Mali.

What helped Salif overcome people's prejudices?

A ambition

B personality

C political power

D talent

Read this sentence from the student's essay.

> Because Salif was from a prestigious royal line, he deserved respect from his family and from society.

What is the meaning of prestigious in this sentence?

A important

B musical

C boring

D artistic

28 **Which word connotes a feeling of power?**

A consider (paragraph 2)

B dominated (paragraph 2)

C embraced (paragraph 4)

D unified (paragraph 2)

29 **What is this passage mostly about?**

A the history of the Malian Empire

B becoming an international star

C the life of a musician

D dealing with prejudice

30 **Why was it a problem for Salif to become a singer?**

A He is a person of royal heritage.

B His family did not support him.

C He is an albino with poor vision.

D He isn't a very good singer.

The Cardiff Giant

1   In 1869, a sensation swept over the small town of Cardiff, New York. A mysterious stone figure o man was found buried on the property of a local farmer named William Newell. The figure was 12 fe tall, with arms and legs twisted in a pose of agony. The surface was marked with tiny pores, like thos human skin, and there were marks like blue veins in the stone. The bottom was grooved, as though it been worn by water over time.

2   Immediately, rumors began spreading about the figure. Many people believed it was the petrified fossil of an ancient giant, evidence of a race of giants who had walked the Earth thousands of years before. Others believed that it was a great, ancient statue buried hundreds of years before. People floc to the site to see the "Cardiff Giant" in his original position, lying in a hole in the ground. In fact, so many people began arriving that Mr. Newell started charging admission!

3   From the start, there were people who did not believe that it was an authentic fossil or an ancient statue. But these doubters were pushed aside by the excited waves of believers who were not ready to change their opinions. Even some scientists came to investigate, and decided the Giant was of ancien origins.

4   Newell began taking in quite a lot of money from displaying the Giant. Soon, the Giant sparked interest of some businessmen in Syracuse. A share in the Giant was sold to them for over $30,000. Th Giant was moved and displayed in Syracuse and New York City. Despite growing doubt among scien and the public, the Giant remained a popular attraction. In fact, the famous showman P.T. Barnum too an interest in the Giant and offered to buy it or lease it for a large sum. However, his offer was refuse he actually had a copy of the Cardiff Giant built. He began displaying the copy and charging admissi Barnum's Giant began drawing even bigger crowds than the original!

5   Meanwhile, more and more scientists came forward with their theories that the stone figure was not truly ancient. Also, suspicious evidence began to surface that the Cardiff Giant was in fact a hoax Eventually, a man came forward and confessed that the whole thing had been his idea. His name was George Hull, and he was Newell's brother-in-law. He had wanted to play a joke on people. He though many people were too gullible—too ready to believe in things just because they wanted to believe the He got the idea for the giant when he was looking at some stone in a mine. He noticed the stone had blue veins in it resembling human veins. He sent a block of the soft stone, called gypsum, to a Germa stone carver. The carver crafted it into a giant human figure, adding tiny holes on the surface to look pores and deep grooves on the back to look like natural erosion. Then, Hull worked with Newell to b the figure secretly on Newell's farm. Later, he had the unwary farm workers dig at the burial site, wh they would find the "buried treasure."

6   Far from being ashamed of his actions, George Hull was very happy and proud to admit that he v behind the whole hoax. He was amused that he had successfully fooled so many people and made so much money in the process!

Which word is most closely related to fooled?

A   interest (paragraph 4)

B   sensation (paragraph 1)

C   hoax (paragraph 5)

D   original (paragraph 4)

Why did George Hull first decide to bury the stone figure?

A   to make money

B   to fool others

C   to test scientists

D   to meet P.T. Barnum

Which word best describes George Hull?

A   dishonest

B   trustworthy

C   friendly

D   honorable

34 **How were William Newell and P.T. Barnum alike?**

A   They both displayed the same giant.

B   They both attracted the same number of people.

C   They both made a lot of money.

D   They both knew that the giant was fake.

35 **What is gypsum?**

A   a soft stone

B   a kind of giant

C   a scientist

D   a kind of joke

36 **What did this story prove?**

A   It is best to be honest with people.

B   Show sorrow when you do something wrong.

C   Ancient treasures can be found anywhere.

D   People will believe just about anything.

Kate Warne: Woman Detective

1   It was a sunny day in August 1856. Allan Pinkerton sat at a desk in his Chicago detective agency. had just finished speaking with a client's wife, and as she exited his office, a slender young woman w brown hair came in. "Good afternoon!" she said cheerfully, "Are you Mr. Allan Pinkerton?"

2   "Yes, I am. How may I help you, miss?"

3   "Well," she replied, nodding toward a paper in her right hand, "I saw your advertisement in the newspaper. I am interested in a job."

4   "A detective? Impossible! It is not the custom to employ women detectives! It can be dangerous work. It requires travel, independence, extreme caution..."

5   "Mr. Pinkerton, let me ask you something. The woman who just left here, what color was her dre

6   Pinkerton thought for a moment, then said, "It was, uh, I believe it was..."

7   "It was light blue, with a matching bonnet trimmed with white lace, and her boots were of brown leather. You see, Mr. Pinkerton, women are excellent observers with an eye for detail. Do you not agr Mr. Pinkerton?"

8   "Well, yes, I suppose you are right, Miss... uh, Miss..."

9   "My name is Kate Warne." She reached out her hand and Mr. Pinkerton shook it.

10   He hired her that day, and the clever young lady did become an excellent detective. But her most important assignment would come in 1861, just before Lincoln's inauguration as president. The Pink Detective Agency was hired to investigate an assassination plot against Lincoln. He was due to arrive train in Baltimore en route to Washington, D.C.

11   Kate first used her detective skills to learn that there was a plot to kill Lincoln at the train station Baltimore. Pinkerton decided that Lincoln's wife and children should travel on the originally schedul train, while Lincoln would secretly take a different train the night before. Kate made the arrangement and she and Pinkerton accompanied him.

12   "Now, Mr. Lincoln," said Kate. "With all due respect, you are quite a recognizable figure. You wi have to remove that tall hat! You are so tall and imposing. Can you bend and pretend you are old and weak?" She demonstrated for Lincoln, who laughed and then imitated her. The three boarded the trai secret, and rode into the night.

13   The next day, Lincoln's family arrived as scheduled in Baltimore, but without Mr. Lincoln himse The would-be assassins were disappointed! And Kate's place as a respected detective was ensured.

Which word best describes Kate Warner?

A   observant

B   deceiving

C   awkward

D   threatened

What was a common belief when this story took place?

A   Women were smarter than men.

B   Women had many opportunities.

C   Women could only do certain jobs.

D   Women were not good secretaries.

Which part of the story is probably fact?

A   Lincoln pretended to be an old lady.

B   Kate Warne was a detective.

C   The clients' wife was wearing a blue dress.

D   The exact conversation actually happened.

40 What is the meaning of <u>en route</u> in paragraph 10?

A   on time

B   in addition to

C   in hope of

D   on the way

41 What is the meaning of <u>imposing</u> in paragraph 12?

A   hidden

B   limited

C   impressive

D   common

42 How did the story end?

A   Pinkerton had doubts about Kate's ability

B   Kate Warne proved she could do the job.

C   Pinkerton wished he had never hired Kate.

D   Kate was unable to do what was expected of her.

To Zorg and Back Again

1   Life on the planet Zorg was great—if you were a Zorgian. If, however, you were a sixth grader named Freddy from Ohio, Earth, well, things were difficult.

2   Freddy met the Zorgians one day in the woods near his house. A timid purple blob, who appeared to be lost, approached him. "Xnghreximuh blurf?" asked the blob. It was speaking its native language from the country Gloop in the western hemisphere of Zorg. Then, he remembered that he was on Eart "¿Dónde estoy?" he tried first, in Spanish. When Freddy replied that he spoke only English, the blob smiled with his trumpet-like snout and said, "Hello! I am Hurbit! I am lost. My parents..."

3   Just then, two large purple blobs emerged from some bushes nearby. Upon seeing their son, they came rolling over, speaking in Gloopish. When they noticed Freddy, they suddenly became extremely polite. "¡Buenos días!" they uttered. Hurbit whispered something to them. They looked surprised, but then said, "Hello!"

4   They explained that they were the Ooo family, who had come to Earth for vacation, accidentally landing in the Ohio woods instead of the Amazon rainforest. They decided they liked Ohio, so Freddy invited them to dinner with his family. The Ooos enjoyed Earth food, and then invited Freddy to trave with them to Zorg. They said he could attend school there and study Gloopish. Freddy was excited: h had never left Ohio before! His parents were nervous, but they decided it was important for their son see the Universe. Freddy's mother drove Freddy and the Ooos to their ship. Then, Freddy said goodb his mother, and the Ooos trumpeted a song of gratitude before they all climbed into the ship and took

5   Things were different on Zorg. It seemed that the only living things on the planet were Zorgians; this reason, Freddy was wondering what Zorgians ate, until Mrs. Ooo arrived at the dinner table with colorful sets of test tubes. "We make all our own food," she boasted. Freddy politely drank the liquid but he felt slightly ill afterwards. He noticed the Ooos' kitchen looked strangely similar to a chemistr laboratory.

6   Most of Zorg looked like laboratories and factories. Hurbit told Freddy that Zorg used to be cove in tall plants and unusual creatures. But the Zorgians built bigger and bigger cities until there was no left except cities. Hurbit explained that's why they like to travel to other planets, to see other kinds of

7   After a few months on Zorg, Freddy seemed depressed. Mrs. Ooo decided it was time to take hin home. She got the spaceship ready, and they took off the next morning. In a flash, they had passed through the Earth's atmosphere and arrived at a wide, paved parking lot. "Here we are!" exclaimed Mrs. Ooo. It was dark, and the lot was empty, but Freddy could see a giant store to the left. To the rig were some very tall apartment buildings. Freddy's heart began pounding as he thought, "What happe to the woods near my house? Had someone replaced them with a city while I was gone? Has Earth become like Zorg?"

8   "Wait a minute," said Mrs. Ooo, pointing to a large sign in Spanish nearby. "How did we end up Mexico City?"

In the story "To Zorg and Back Again," what is Gloopish?

A   a language

B   a country

C   a person

D   an activity

How did the story end?

A   Freddy loves living on the planet Zorg.

B   Freddy wishes he were back home.

C   Freddy is baking cookies with the Ooos.

D   Freddy is working in a chemistry laboratory.

Why does Freddy become depressed on Zorg?

A   He doesn't like Mrs. Ooo's food.

B   He doesn't like Hurbit.

C   He doesn't speak Gloopish.

D   He misses life in Ohio.

46   What genre of writing is this story?

A   folktale

B   historical fiction

C   science fiction

D   poetry

47   Which is an example of figurative language?

A   trumpeted a song of gratitude

B   Hello! I am Hurbit!

C   four colorful sets of test tubes

D   things were difficult

48   At the end of the story, why did Freddy's heart begin pounding?

A   He thought Earth had changed.

B   He didn't like the Ooos' food.

C   He thought he was sick.

D   He didn't want to go home.

Parrots Around the World

1   You've seen them in cartoons, on pirates' shoulders, and maybe in pet stores and homes. But how much do you know about the different varieties of parrots?

2   Parrots belong to the order of birds called *Psittaciformes*. They can be found in warm and tropica climates around the world. All parrots have a curved beak, which is good for opening seeds and nuts. They also have zygodactyl feet, which means that they have two front-facing toes and two back-facin toes on each foot. Most parrots are brightly colored, but some can be white, grey, or black.

3   The largest parrot is the Hyacinth Macaw, which is bright blue, and can be up to 40 inches (100 centimeters) long. This and many other types of macaws are native to Mexico, Central Ameri and South America. They are all endangered species because of illegal hunting and pet trade.

4   In New Zealand, there is a yellowish-green parrot called the Kakapo. The Kakapo is unusual bec: it cannot fly! Before Europeans arrived and began living on the island, there were no predators there hunt the heavy, flightless birds. But the colonists brought cats and rats, which hunted the Kakapos. T there are almost no Kakapos left.

5   Many other types of parrots can be found throughout Asia, Africa, Australia, and Central and So America. They vary in size, color, and other features, but they all share some basic traits, including a beauty and intelligence that have made them popular pets for centuries.

Read this encyclopedia entry.

Jane Goodall (b. 1931, London, England) — *primatologist, anthropologist, conservationist*

1   In 1960, a woman named Jane Goodall went to Tanzania to observe chimpanzees. No woman ha ever gone into the wilds of Africa to observe animals before. But her research was new and different other ways, too. Usually, scientists assigned numbers to the animals they observed. However, Gooda gave her chimps names. She thought that they were individuals with distinct personalities. She also approached them slowly and made social and physical contact with them. This is something else that scientists do not normally do.

2   In her many years of research, Goodall discovered several surprising facts about chimps. She fou that they make simple tools to get food. They form lasting family bonds and are capable of compassi They are also capable of war and great violence.

3   Goodall has been both praised and criticized for her tactics. She is widely admired for her many new and important findings about chimpanzee society. She helped people to see chimps in a new wa But some criticize her for becoming emotionally involved with her subjects. Some also think that sh influenced the results of her observations by making contact with the chimps and interfering with the natural life.

Animals That Talk

We know that animals use sounds, body language, and other signals to communicate with each other. But can animals communicate ideas and feelings, like humans do? Let's read about two scientists who try to answer this question.

ny Patterson and Koko

Dr. Francine (Penny) Patterson began working with a one-year-old baby gorilla named Koko in 1972. She began teaching Koko American Sign Language. Many of the signs were adapted for the special shape of gorillas' hands. Since the program began, Koko has learned to use over 1,000 different signs and to understand over 2,000 spoken words. One notable thing about Koko's use of language is her ability to use signs creatively. For example, she once used the words "finger" and "bracelet"—"finger-bracelet"—to refer to a ring. She had not learned the sign for "ring," so she found a new way to say it. Another notable thing is Koko's seeming ability to convey her feelings. Koko adopted and cared for a pet kitten, which she named "All Ball." One day, All Ball was hit by a car. Koko signed the words "sad" and "cry." Patterson said Koko cried for two days afterward.

Many people believe that these examples show Koko's capacity for abstract thought. They think that Koko is using language to express feelings and ideas. However, some scientists think differently. They believe that Koko's handlers may be misreading Koko's signs or adding meaning to them.

Pepperberg and Alex

Perhaps Koko's achievements are not so surprising. After all, gorillas and other primates are closely related to humans. But what about other kinds of animals, like birds?

Parrots can mimic human speech. But can they understand the words they say? Or are they only repeating sounds? Dr. Irene Pepperberg was convinced that parrots were more intelligent than people thought. Her 30 years of work with an African Grey parrot named Alex has shown it. Dr. Pepperberg bought Alex from a pet store in 1977. With Dr. Pepperberg's special teaching methods, Alex learned over 00 words. According to Pepperberg's research, he could identify 50 objects, five shapes, six colors, quantities up to six, and certain materials. He also understood concepts of size and likeness. For example, he could pick out a blue triangle from a tray of objects on request. Then he could say if it was made of paper, wood, or wool by picking it up and examining it. He had even begun to learn to associate sounds with letters!

As with Koko, scientists disagree about Alex's abilities. Was he actually using language and abstract thought? Or was he simply reacting to his trainers? The debate continues about whether or not animals can truly use language. However, even skeptical scientists admit that Koko and Alex are clearly intelligent. Drs. Patterson and Pepperberg have certainly shown that there's more to animals than many people thought!

49 How are Kakapos like Hyacinth Macaws?

A   They are the same color.

B   They are endangered.

C   They are native to Mexico.

D   They are unable to fly.

50 Read this sentence from "Parrots Around the World."

> They are all endangered species because of illegal hunting and pet trade.

What is the meaning of illegal in the sentence?

A   within one's rights

B   following local customs

C   not lawful

D   impossible to do

51 How is Jane Goodall different from most other scientists?

A   She has been recognized for her achievements.

B   She established a personal relationship with the animals.

C   She educates others about what she has learned.

D   She assigned numbers to the animals.

52 What is this encyclopedia entry mostl about?

A   how chimpanzees behave

B   conducting scientific information

C   a dedicated scientist

D   conservation education

53 Where would you most likely find information about Jane Goodall in an encyclopedia?

A   under primatologist

B   under Tanzania

C   under archaeology

D   under wildlife conservation

What is the message of the passage, "Animals That Talk"?

A   Some animals have an ability to communicate.

B   Sign language is helpful in training animals.

C   Findings of scientists are questioned by many.

D   Gorillas are more intelligent than parrots.

How was Koko different from Alex?

A   She could understand the spoken word.

B   She communicated her feelings.

C   She was studied by a dedicated scientist.

D   She was actually able to speak.

Why did Dr. Pepperberg decide to study Alex?

A   She wanted to teach him the complex language of humans.

B   She wanted to save him from the conditions of the pet store.

C   She wanted to prove the intelligence of parrots.

D   She wanted to teach him how to sound out new words.

57 **Who would most likely benefit by studying the work of these scientists?**

A   owners of pet stores

B   visitors of zoos

C   teachers of sign language

D   animal trainers

58 **What is a main idea found in all three passages?**

A   People should not interfere in the lives of animals.

B   Animal welfare is the responsibility of people.

C   People are often criticized for their work with animals.

D   Human behavior affects animal behavior.

59 **What are all three passages about?**

A   dedicated scientists

B   preserving wildlife

C   intelligent animals

D   animals as pets

The Waterville Observer
July 20, 1988

Doubleview Drive-In Closes!

1   After 40 years in operation, the Doubleview Drive-In Theater will be airing its last two features, *Die Hard* and *Coming to America*, on Saturday, July 30 at dusk. Frank and Heloise Murphy, owners the private outdoor cinema since 1956, announced the closing just this week. They are saddened, but resigned. "We know times have changed," remarked Heloise. "People just don't go to drive-ins anym Hundreds of customers do still come every week, pay admission at the gate, and park their cars in a next to a mini-speaker, where they can enjoy new releases on a giant outdoor screen from the privacy their own vehicle. "It's just not enough," complained Frank Murphy.

2   About a mile from the drive-in, a large indoor cinema complex opened just two years ago. With comfortable seats and state-of-the-art sound system, the cinema has done a booming business. "We j can't compete," explains Heloise.

3   Heloise and Frank inherited the theater from Heloise's father Hal Avery, who passed away in 19 when Heloise was 25 years old. "Now I guess it's time for us to retire," she says. The couple plans t their home and move to Florida before the winter. As for the theater, no plans have been made yet fo lot it stands on.

The Waterville Observer
March 5, 2008

Parks, Not Condos

1   As a concerned grandparent and longtime Waterville resident, I am quite upset that our town is talking about developing condominiums on the site of the old Doubleview Drive-In. Many residents agree that the best use of this vacant lot is a park.

2   When I was a kid, there was plenty of outdoor space to play in. Since then, most of that land has been lost to houses, malls, and highways. Nowadays, kids don't have a lot of space to play in. More an more kids are playing video games and watching TV. Another reason to have a park is for aesthetic and environmental reasons. Trees, grass, and flowers can beautify our town, while also contributing to our air. Condos will only contribute to pollution and the crowding of our town with more buildings and car

3   A park is a place where people can get together for family picnics, community events, and celebrations. I know that the town would like to gain the profits from selling the land to developers. believe that a healthy, happy community is more important than money. New condos would attract n people to Waterville, but if we lose this opportunity to improve the quality of our town, we would be losing a big reason for people to want to stay here.

What is the meaning of <u>resigned</u> in paragraph 1 of "Doubleview Drive-in Closes!"?

A   willing to fight for

B   unable to understand

C   accepting of the fact

D   determined to change

What did the drive-in have that the cinema complex didn't?

A   new releases

B   admission prices

C   a chance for privacy

D   a giant screen

What is the meaning of <u>booming</u> in paragraph 2?

A   successful

B   loud

C   failing

D   ordinary

63   **What does the last sentence lead us to believe?**

A   The outdoor cinema will be knocked down.

B   The outdoor cinema will be remodeled.

C   Another cinema complex will be built.

D   The cinema complex will also close down.

64   **What happened on the date July 20, 1988?**

A   The outdoor cinema closed.

B   The cinema complex opened.

C   The reporter spoke to the Murphys.

D   The article appeared in the paper.

65   **Which word or phrase is related to the word <u>modern</u>?**

A   inherited (paragraph 3)

B   state-of-the-art (paragraph 2)

C   retire (paragraph 3)

D   compete (paragraph 2)

66 Where would the editorial "Parks, Not Condos" appear in the newspaper?

A   in the sports section

B   on the world news page

C   on the comics page

D   on the opinion page

67 What is the author in favor of?

A   the town making more money

B   people living healthier lives

C   attracting more people to the town

D   having people move out of the town

68 How was life years ago different than today in Waterville?

A   The town was more beautiful.

B   There was more development.

C   There was more outdoor space.

D   There were more public parks.

69 What is the meaning of <u>contribute</u> in paragraph 2?

A   to get along with others

B   to supply for publishing

C   to offer one's opinion

D   to have a share in something

70 Who does the author say agrees with

A   other residents

B   the mayor of the town

C   the Town Council

D   the developer

71 How are "Doubleview Drive-In Close and "Parks, Not Condos" alike?

A   They are both about people who are upset.

B   They are both about how things cha over time.

C   They appeared in the paper on in the same day.

D   They are written by the same perso

● Vocabulary From the Reading

Use with student book page 6.

> **Key Vocabulary**
>
> | | |
> |---|---|
> | anxious | pace |
> | approach | reputation |
> | exhausted | rupture |

A. Match each word to its definition.

Example: ___*c*___ break open

1. _____ nervous   a. approach

2. _____ rate of speed   b. anxious

3. _____ come closer   c. ~~rupture~~

                     d. reputation

4. _____ very tired   e. pace

5. _____ public image   f. exhausted

B. Complete the paragraph using the Key Vocabulary words.

    At school, I had a ___*reputation*___ for being a good student—I always got **As** on my exams. However, my first year of geometry was different. The _____ of the class was too fast—I could not finish all the homework. I started getting very low grades. I wanted to _____ the exam with a calm mind, but I started getting very _____ because I didn't want to do badly. I studied so hard every night I thought my brain was going to _____! Finally, the exam day arrived and I did my best. I was relieved when I got my exam back and saw a big, red **A** at the top, but I was too _____ to celebrate—I fell asleep as soon as I got home!

C. Write about a new or difficult experience you had. Use four Key Vocabulary words.

_____

_____

_____

_____

_____

Name _____ Date _____

● Reading Strategy

Use with student book page 7.

Relate Your Own Experiences to a Reading

When you **relate your own experience to a reading,** you think about how your experience is similar to someone else's. After you read, it is helpful to **summarize** your responses to show how you relate to the reading.

Academic Vocabulary for the Reading Strategy	
Word	**Explanation**
relate	to connect
summarize	to make a summary, or a brief account of a reading

Read the passage about Nargess and her family. Then complete the chart.

1 The most difficult challenge for my family and me when we first moved to this country was communication. My father knew some English, but my mother, brother, and I did not speak a word. And then, there was the alphabet! We only knew the Farsi alphabet, so reading signs and labels was very hard.

2 My brother and I started English classes right away. When we came home each day, we taught our mother what we learned. This helped us practice, too. We put all the letters on flash cards and reviewed them over and over again. We wrote labels in big letters and taped them to things all over the house—TABLE, CHAIR, CUP, RICE, etc. My father laughed when he saw them!

3 My brother and I had trouble making friends at first because we were shy. Eventually, my brother joined the soccer team, and I joined the school chorus. Singing in English helped me a lot with my accent and self-confidence. My brother made friends on his team, and talking to them helped his English, too. By the end of our second year, we had many friends we could talk to. Meanwhile, our mother's English had become good enough to get a job at a store!

1. What major challenge does Nargess face? Summarize how she responds to the challenge.

_____

_____

_____

_____

2. What major challenge are you facing? How are you responding to it?

_____

_____

_____

_____

Name _____ Date _____

● Text Genre

Use with student book page 8.

Autobiographical Short Story

Autobiographical Short Story	
characters	people in a story
conflict	a struggle between two opposing forces
plot	events in a story that happen in a certain order
description	vivid details that add interest to the narrative

Read the autobiographical short story by Becky. Then answer the questions below.

1 I grew up in a typical Anglo-American household. In middle school, I met a Mexican-American girl named Gaby. We became close friends.

2 One day, Gaby invited me to a family party. I could not believe how crowded and lively the house was. People were dancing to rhythmic Mexican music while Gaby's mother served homemade Mexican food. I had fun, but afterwards I began to feel anxious. Gaby was coming to *my* house for a family birthday the following Friday. What would Gaby think of *my* party? There would only be a few people sitting around a table with a simple cake.

3 Gaby came to the house that Friday dressed in her best clothes. My family was in jeans and T-shirts. I was sure Gaby would feel uncomfortable, but to my surprise, she began making conversation with everyone. She even brought a CD of Mexican music. Gaby taught us how to dance to it! We all danced to American music afterwards, and everyone had fun, especially me.

1. Who are the main characters? _____

2. What is the conflict? _____

   _____

3. List four main events of the plot.

   a. _____

   b. _____

   c. _____

   d. _____

4. Give two examples of vivid description in the story.

   a. _____

   b. _____

Name _____ Date _____

● Reading Comprehension

Use with student book page 18.

Academic Vocabulary for the Reading Comprehension Questions	
Word	**Explanation**
analyze	to examine something to understand what it is and means, or to study
predict	to say what will happen in the future

A. **Retell the story.** Summarize the story "Making Connections" in your own words. Include the main events of the plot.

_____

_____

_____

_____

_____

B. **Write your response.** Analyze Panchito's response to the book his teacher gives him to read. How does his attitude change toward the book? Is there a book or story that has affected you this strongly? Explain.

_____

_____

_____

_____

_____

C. **Assess the reading strategy.** Were you able to relate to Panchito's experiences? How did the Reading Strategy chart on page 18 of your book help you do this? Name two things that you discovered you had in common with Panchito.

_____

_____

_____

Name _____ Date _____

● Literary Element

Use with student book page 19.

First-Person Narrative

> A **first-person narrative** is a story told by the main character who uses the first-person pronoun "I" to refer to him or herself.

Read the story excerpt. Then answer the questions.

1 It was 18 years earlier that my mother left Albania. She didn't talk to me much about why she left. In fact, she never talked much at all. She quietly went about her daily business, telling me only what she needed to tell me. When she looked at me, I could see a great love in her eyes, but I also saw a deep sadness.

2 One day while she was cooking, I told her that I wanted to study in Albania that summer and find the village where she was born. She suddenly stopped peeling the potato. She looked worried but said nothing for several minutes. "Donjeta," she said firmly as she looked up, "there is nothing for you there." The intense love, fear, and determination in her dark eyes stopped me from responding. She looked down and began peeling again, this time almost angrily ripping the skin from the potato. I understood in that moment that the road to the heart of my mother's story was going to be a long one.

1. Go back and underline all the clues that tell you this is a first-person narrative.

2. What is the narrator's name? How do you know?

   _____

3. What does the narrator want to find out? Why is it difficult?

   _____

   _____

4. Describe the narrator's relationship with her mother.

   _____

   _____

5. How do you think the story might be different if told by someone outside of the story?

   _____

   _____

Name _____   Date _____

● **Vocabulary From the Reading**   *Use with student book page 20.*

┌───┐
│ **Key Vocabulary**   │
│ export   template   │
│ global   │
└───┘

A. Complete the chart. Write your own definition of each Key Vocabulary word.

Example: export   *send goods to other countries*

Key Word	My Definition
global	1. _____
template	2. _____

B. Complete each sentence with a Key Vocabulary word.

Example: The secretary uses a _____*template*_____ to type her letters, so they are all in the same standard format.

1. Many large businesses are _____; they make and sell products all over the world.

2. The workers in the shoe factory use a _____ to cut the pieces correctly.

3. China and Japan _____ many manufactured products to other countries.

C. Use each of the Key Vocabulary words to make three sentences about your country of origin.

1. _____

    _____

2. _____

    _____

3. _____

    _____

Name ————————————————————— Date ——————————————

● Reading Strategy

Use with student book page 21.

Relate Your Own Experiences to a Reading

> **Relating your own experiences** to an idea, event, or character in a reading can help you increase your comprehension.

As you read about this market, look for foods, products, events, or services that you recognize. Can you find them in your country of origin or in your local community? What is your connection to the items? Organize your notes in the chart.

1 The Midtown Global Market in Minneapolis, Minnesota, is a place where people of all cultures can go to eat, browse, and shop. The indoor market, host to over fifty businesses, shows the cultural diversity of Minneapolis.

2 In the market, you can find groceries imported from the Middle East, Latin America, and other regions of the world. Specialty food and craft items from Scandinavia are on sale right next to *saris* or *salwar kamis* from India, Hmong textiles from Southeast Asia, or Andean sweaters and ponchos from Ecuador. If you are hungry, you will find West Indian, East African, Vietnamese, Italian, and Mexican prepared foods to take out or to eat at one of the many tables at the market. No matter what you want—*falafel, gyros, tamales,* Jamaican jerk chicken, sushi, burgers, or *lefsa*—you will find it there. You can buy fresh fish, meat, cheese, and bakery items such as baguette*s* or *tres leches* cakes. There is also a seasonal farmers' market with locally grown fruits and vegetables.

3 From 7:00 A.M. to 8:00 P.M. daily, the Global Market is an important gathering place for native Minnesotans and immigrants alike.

Fill in the chart. In the third column, write the dictionary definition for each word or a personal connection you have with the item.

Product, Food, Event, Service	Country or Region of Origin	Definition or Connection
Example: baguette	France	*Definition:* loaf of bread *Connection:* We eat these in Algeria, too.
1. _____	_____	
2. _____	_____	
3. _____	_____	

Name _____ Date _____

● Text Genre

Use with student book page 21.

Informational Text: Magazine Article

Magazine Article		
Feature	**Purpose**	**Appearance**
photographs and illustrations	allow readers to see new or interesting images related to the article	may be color or black-and-white; may appear anywhere in the article
segments or sections	break the article into parts that relate to the article's subject matter	may begin with a heading or a space that separates it from the section before it

Read the magazine article excerpt below. Then answer the questions.

1 For travelers on a tight budget, Paris may seem scary, but there are many options for spending your nights without spending all your savings. The Aloha Hostel in Montparnasse is just one of the many possibilities.

2 There is plenty to see and do in the city without spending a dime. A walk along the river Seine offers the opportunity appreciate the city's magnificent architecture. Or you can take a stroll through the park at Tuileries.

3 In Paris, you do not need to eat expensively to eat well. For example, at a neighborhood bistro you can get a good meal and a good deal.

1. What title do you think would best fit this magazine article? What type of magazine do you think it would appear in?

   _____

2. What heading would you give each section of this article?

   1 _____

   2 _____

   3 _____

3. What photograph(s) do you think would fit each section of the article? Do you think color or black-and-white would work better? Why?

   1 _____

   2 _____

   3 _____

Name _____ Date _____

● Reading Comprehension

Use with student book page 27.

A. **Retell the story.** Summarize the article "Words Around the World." What do you think the main idea is?

_____

_____

_____

_____

_____

B. **Write your response.** Analyze the way in which the global economy changes language all over the world. What do you predict might happen to English in the future? To other world languages? Why?

_____

_____

_____

_____

_____

C. **Assess the reading strategy.** How does making personal connections to the content improve your understanding of the text? Give an example.

_____

_____

_____

_____

_____

Name _____ Date _____

● **Spelling** *Use with student book page 27.*

Words with the Same Sounds but Different Spellings

The words **you're** and **your** and the words **it's** and **its** have the same sound. When you write, be sure you use the correct spelling.

Word	Meaning	Example
you're	you are (contraction)	**You're** from Mexico, right?
your	belonging to you (possessive adjective)	Is that **your** composition?
it's	it is (contraction)	I like *The Grapes of Wrath*. **It's** a great book.
its	belonging to it (possessive adjective)	English is a diverse language. Many of **its** words have foreign origins.

A. Read the sentences and circle the correct word.

Example: I want to hear (you're /(your)) opinion about the book.

1. (It's / Its) interesting to study word origins.

2. I noticed the book was thick when I ran my fingers along (it's / its) spine.

3. A story is autobiographical if you write about (you're / your) experiences.

4. The word *pajamas* has (it's / its) origins in the Hindi language.

5. (You're / Your) late for class!

B. Fill in the blanks with **you're, your, it's,** or **its.**

Example: _____It's_____ a new house, but _____its_____ design is old-fashioned.

1. Our country has many native languages, but _____ official language is English.

2. English is very widely spoken. _____ the common language of international business.

3. _____ a good writer, Panchito. _____ story is very interesting.

4. _____ calling _____ uncle in Ghana at this

   hour, Florence? _____ almost midnight there!

Milestones C • Copyright © Heinle

Name _____ Date _____

● Writing Conventions

Use with student book page 27.

Punctuation: Quotation Marks to Refer to a Word

One use of **quotation marks** is to set off a word you are defining or referencing. Don't use quotation marks with a word that is a meaningful part of the sentence.

The word "sandwich" is understood in most non-English speaking parts of the world.	Used as reference
I usually eat a sandwich for lunch.	Used with meaning

A. Rewrite the sentences. Add quotation marks where needed. Put commas and periods inside the quotation marks.

Example: What is the origin of the word chocolate?

What is the origin of the word "chocolate"?

1. The words entrée, liaison, and crêpe come from French. _____

   _____

2. Arturo has difficulty pronouncing refrigerator. _____

   _____

3. Do you know what template means? _____

   _____

4. He whispered Rosebud just before he died. _____

   _____

B. Write a paragraph of four sentences. Explain the meaning of two interesting words from your native language. Then talk about two words in the English language that you have had trouble with.

   _____

   _____

   _____

   _____

Name _____ Date _____

● Vocabulary Development

Use with student book page 29.

Greek and Latin Root Words

Here are some Greek and Latin roots:

Root	Meaning	English Word
scrib	write	description, transcribe
gress	walk, go	progress, digress
geo	earth	geometry, geography
phone	sound, voice	telephone, phonetics
graph	write	

Now look at these prefixes and suffixes:

Prefixes and Suffixes	Meaning
trans-	across
pro-	for, forward
-logy	study of

A. Based on the roots, prefixes, and suffixes in the charts above, guess what the following words mean. Then look them up in a dictionary to confirm your predictions.

Word	My Guess at Definition	Dictionary definition
Example: transcribe	write across	copy in writing from one place to another
1. progress		
2. geography		
3. phonology		
4. transgress		

B. Write a sentence using the words in exercise **A.**

1. _____

2. _____

3. _____

4. _____

Name _____ Date _____

● Grammar

Use with student book pages 30–31.

Subject-Verb Agreement in the Simple Present Tense

Subjects and verbs should agree in number.

Subject-Verb Agreement			
	Subject	**Verb**	
Singular Subject	The student	sits	here.
Plural Subject	The students	sit	here.

A. Put the verbs and nouns from the list below into the correct category in the chart.

Nouns:		**Verbs:**	
workers	~~template~~	use	carries
children	language	needs	say
paper	articles	process	fixes

Singular Nouns	Plural Nouns	Singular Verbs	Plural Verbs
Example: template			

B. Circle the correct answer. Make sure the verb agrees with the subject.

Example: Many business people ((speak)/ speaks) English.

1. Pancho (go / goes) to school at 7:00 A.M.

2. Mama (dress / dresses) Trampita in clothes from the dump.

3. The students (study / studies) very hard every day.

4. The teacher (help / helps) them with English.

5. English (borrow / borrows) many words from other languages.

6. Other languages sometimes (borrow / borrows) words from English, too.

7. Many people around the world (use / uses) the English word "OK."

8. English (serve / serves) as a lingua franca for many people.

Name _____ Date _____

Use the present tense to talk about things that are generally true or happen often. Notice the subject-verb agreement in the sentence below.

                 subject   **verb**

Generally true: The sun always rises in the east.

                 subject   **verb**

Happens often: Motorcycle riders wear safety helmets to protect their heads.

C. Write complete sentences with the subjects and verbs given. Complete them using real information. Use the correct present tense forms of the verbs.

Example: the man / want   *The young man wants a new pair of sneakers.*

1. my teacher / teach   _____

2. my friends / watch   _____

3. my country / export   _____

4. my classmates / write   _____

5. my favorite book / tell   _____

D. Read the paragraph and use editing marks to correct any mistakes in subject-verb agreement.

    Mrs. Wu's computer class teach students to build Web sites. Beginner

students use a special template on their screen to get started. The template help

them know where to type certain information. Marlon Frantz says the class

is difficult, but Adam Lopez and Thoai Nguyen thinks that it is very easy. This

week, the class research the history of the Internet. The school library carries

many books on the subject, but the kids prefers to use Google and Wikipedia.

Name _____ Date _____

● Grammar Expansion
Compound Subjects and Modified Subjects

The verb should agree with the subject, even if another noun is closer to it.

A **compound subject** is a subject made up of more than one person, place, or thing:
   Tricia, Jane, and Mark
In the following sentence, the subject of the first verb includes three people, so the first verb has to agree with the plural subject. But the second subject is just one person, so the verb is singular.
   <u>Tricia, Jane, and Mark</u> **go** to Spanish class, but <u>Jesse</u> **goes** to Arabic class.

A **modified subject** is a subject with adjectives or phrases describing it:
   Subject modified by adjectives: the big, fat, hairy, brown <u>spiders</u>
   Subject modified by a phrase: the <u>price</u> of lemons
Make sure the verb agrees only with the subject and not another word:
   The <u>price</u> of lemons **varies** from store to store. (The verb agrees with *price*, not *lemons*. The price varies, not the lemons.)

A. Underline the subject in each sentence.

Example: the shiny new <u>pennies</u> from the bank

1. The new exchange students from Taiwan arrive tomorrow.
2. The delicious Greek butter cookies are all gone!
3. The girl with red hair and green eyes is my sister.
4. The number of foreign words in English is surprising.

B. Fill in the verb form that agrees with the subject.

Example: The unpleasant smell of rotten grapes __fills__ the air. (fill)

1. Dimitrios, Georgia, and Sarantis _____ from Greece. (come)
2. The global use of computers _____ every year. (increase)
3. My textbook and my computer _____ me improve my English. (help)
4. My tall, attractive classmate with glasses _____ me, too. (help)

C. Write one sentence using compound subjects and one using modified subjects. Write about people or places in your community.

1. _____
2. _____

Name _____ Date _____

● Grammar Expansion

Yes / No Questions and Negative Statements in the Present Tense

Singular Question in the Present Tense			
Question	**does**	**singular subject**	**verb**
	Does	Mr. Siteki	speak English?

Singular Answer in the Present Tense			
Answer	**singular subject**	**does + not**	**verb**
	Mr. Siteki	does not	speak English.

Plural Question in the Present Tense			
Question	**do**	**plural subject**	**verb**
	Do	the businessmen	speak English?

Plural Answer in the Present Tense			
Answer	**plural subject**	**do + not**	**verb**
	The businessmen	do not	speak English.

A. Rewrite these sentences to make them negative.

Example: Panchito does all of his homework.

Panchito does not do all of his homework. _____

1. Jessica studies German. _____

2. The students finish the exam. _____

3. Mrs. Lin tries to learn English. _____

B. Complete the questions.

Example: __Do__ you __like__ peas?

Yes, I like peas.

1. A: _____ Elena _____ dance classes?

   B: Yes, she takes dance classes with me.

2. A: _____ Todd and Anika _____ about their grades?

   B: No, they do not worry about their grades. They are straight A students!

44

Name _____ Date _____

● Writing Assignment
Personal Narrative

Use with student book pages 32–33.

A. First, brainstorm your topic—a time when you learned something about yourself. When you have narrowed down your topic, go on to Exercise B.

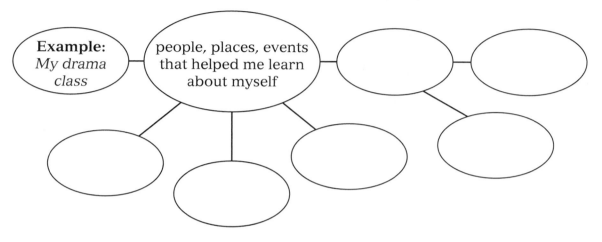

B. Create a timeline of events leading up to the moment you learned something about yourself.

1. _____

First, _____
_____
_____
_____
_____

2. _____

Then, _____
_____
_____
_____
_____

3. _____

Later, _____
_____
_____
_____
_____

4. _____

Finally, _____
_____
_____
_____

5. _____

When it was all over,
_____
_____
_____
_____

6. _____

At last, _____
_____
_____
_____
_____

Name _____ Date _____

● Writing Assignment
Writing Support

Use with student book page 33.

> **Grammar: Capitalization of Proper Nouns and Adjectives**
> All **proper nouns** need to be capitalized. Proper nouns include the names of people and places. Some proper nouns describe time. Some refer to nationality. Names of academic courses are also proper nouns.

Names	Places	Times	People/Languages	Courses
Ben	Victory Park	April	French	English Language Arts
Miss Bell	March School	Thursday	Austrian	Algebra 1
Mamá	Mexico	January	Chinese	American History

A. Read each noun. If it needs to be capitalized, rewrite it on the line provided. If it does not need to be capitalized, write *OK* on the line.

Example: city _____ OK _____

1. today _____

2. wednesday _____

3. teacher _____

4. mr. ellis _____

5. texas _____

6. country _____

7. april _____

8. venezuelan _____

B. Correct the capitalization in the following paragraph. Use editing marks.

  I go to the springfield public library almost every day after school to study. My favorite subject is ancient history, but I also study other subjects. On fridays, however, I usually go straight home because there is usually something fun to do. I sometimes go to the korean restaurant near my house, or I meet my friend alicia and we go to the movies. There is a big cinema at the belleview mall, and in the spring there are free movies outdoors at evans park. I will miss the movies this weekend because my family and I are traveling to new york to visit my older brother's college—cornell university.

46

Name _____ Date _____

● Writing Assignment
Revising Activity

Use with student book page 33.

Read each revision tip. Then rewrite the sentences to make them better.

Revision Tip # 1: Add vivid details to hold the reader's interest. Use descriptive adjectives and phrases.

First Try	A Better Way to Say It
Example: My coach was great.	My energetic and talented soccer coach was important to me.
1. It is an interesting book.	
2. The waitress serves the food.	
3. My teacher helps me.	
4. It was a cold day.	

Revision Tip # 2: Use time and sequence words to clarify the order of events.

First Try	A Better Way to Say It
Example: My mother grabbed my hand. She pulled me out of the restaurant. (sequence)	My mother grabbed my hand. Then she pulled me out of the restaurant.
Example: I step into the street. I see a truck coming straight at me. (same time)	As I step into the street, I see a truck coming straight at me.
1. The principal walked into the room. He closed the door. He turned and looked at me.	
2. I woke up. I smelled smoke. I ran into the living room. I saw the curtains were on fire.	
3. My parents made the arrangements. They took me to the airport.	
4. Natalie arrives at our house. She stays for three weeks. She comes back to stay for a whole year.	

Name _____   Date _____

● Writing Assignment
Editing Activity

Use with student book page 27.

Read the story and find the mistakes. Mark the mistakes using the editing marks on page 455. Then rewrite the story correctly.

Tomorrow is march 14, a very important day. Its my best friend kim's birthday. Usually her parents gives her a small party on her actual birthday, but this year is special. She doesnt know that we are having a big surprise party for her tonight. The mexican restaurant on the corner of elm street and center avenue offer large tables for parties, and on saturday nights they have live mariachi music. The word mariachi originally comes from the french word mariage, which means marriage, but mariachi music, with it's loud horns and lively beats, is fun for any celebration. Its going to be a fun party!

_____

_____

_____

_____

_____

_____

_____

_____

_____

_____

_____

_____

_____

Name _____ Date _____

● Vocabulary From the Reading

Use with student book page 38.

> **Key Vocabulary**
>
> concept   notation
> equation   universal
> equivalent

A. Read the clues. Fill in the missing Key Vocabulary words.

Example: the same thing: e q u (i) v (a) l e n t

1. abbreviation; representation in symbols: ◯_ _ _ _ _◯_

2. a mathematical formula: ◯_ _ _ _ _◯◯

3. an idea: ◯_ _ _ _ _◯

4. shared, known, or understood by everyone: _ _ _◯_◯◯_ _

B. Now write the circled letters in the spaces below.

Circled letters: ◯◯◯◯◯◯◯◯◯◯◯◯◯

Unscramble the letters to make a word that means "dialogue: type of

communication between people." __ __ __ __ __ __ __ __ __ __ __ __ __

C. Answer the questions below.

1. Name one common type of notation that people use. (Example: scientific

    notation) _____

    _____

2. Give one example of an equation. _____

3. Define the phrase **universal concept.** Think of one example of a universal
    concept. Explain the concept and why it is universal.

    _____

    _____

    _____

    _____

Name _____ Date _____

● Reading Strategy

Use with student book page 39.

Recognize Textbook Features

> Textbook pages **consist** of special features. It is important to **recognize textbook features**. When you analyze these features, you can learn new information faster and easier. When you read a textbook, **restate** the information and **define** each feature.

Academic Vocabulary for the Reading Strategy		
Word	**Explanation**	
consist	to be made up of; to be composed of	
restate	to say something in a new way	
define	to give the meaning of	

Read the textbook excerpt. Describe the features and why they are helpful.

Section 1.6 Math and Music

Music is the pleasure the human mind experiences from counting without being aware that it is counting. —Gottfried Leibniz (1646–1716)

Some people don't enjoy math, but almost everyone enjoys music. Did you know that music is actually math?

To hear songs in 2/4, 3/4, and 4/4 time, go to the Web page at **www.gbpress.com/ mathandmusic**!

In Section 1.2, you learned about fractions. Fractions can help you understand music. Written music consists of **bars**. Let's start with a song in 4/4 time. Think of a bar of music in 4/4 time as one unit that can be divided into four counts, or four **quarters.** A note held for four beats is a whole note because the bar consists of four beats. A note held for one count is a quarter note because four of them would complete a bar. Look at Figure 1.22 to see how the fractions add up to a whole in each bar.

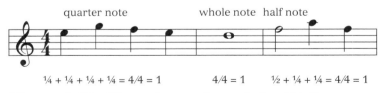

¼ + ¼ + ¼ + ¼ = 4/4 = 1   4/4 = 1   ½ + ¼ + ¼ = 4/4 = 1

Figure 1.22: Three bars of music in 4/4 time

Section Check-Up

○ **Define** "quarter note."
○ Explain Gottfried Leibniz's quote.

Text Feature	How It Looks	How It Helps Me
Example: diagram	bars of music	visualize concepts

Name _____   Date _____

● Text Genre
Textbook

Use with student book page 40.

Textbooks	
facts	information such as dates, events, and numbers
lessons	information to be learned with activities
visual aids	pictures, drawings and charts to help you understand what you are reading

Read the social studies textbook excerpt. Then answer the questions.

Discovering Senegal

1 Senegal is located on the West African coast, between Mauritania and Guinea-Bissau. A former French colony, the official language of Senegal is French, but other languages commonly spoken are Wolof, Pulaar, Jolo, and Mandinka.

2 The Wolof ethnic group comprises 43% of the population, while 23.8% are Pulaar, 14.7% are Serer, 3.7% are Jola, 3% are Mandinka, and 1.1% are Soninke. Only 1% of the population is European or Lebanese, and 9.4% have other ethnic origins.

1. List two **facts** from the reading.

   Fact 1: _____

   Fact 2: _____

2. What is the topic of the **lesson?**

   _____

   _____

   _____

3. What visual aids could improve your understanding of the lesson?

   _____

   _____

   _____

   _____

   _____

Name _____ Date _____

● **Reading Comprehension**   *Use with student book page 47.*

Academic Vocabulary for the Reading Comprehension Questions		
Word	Explanation	
comprehend	to understand the meaning of something	
context	the information surrounding a word or phrase that determines exactly how it is meant	

A. **Retell the story.** Restate the main ideas and lessons from "Mathematically Speaking."

_____

_____

_____

_____

_____

B. **Write your response.** Which textbook features helped you the most in comprehending the reading? Explain.

_____

_____

_____

_____

_____

C. **Assess the reading strategy.** How does context help in understanding text? Did the context of the reading help you understand it better? Explain.

_____

_____

_____

_____

Name _____ Date _____

● Text Element
Visual Aids

Use with student book page 47.

> Visual aids are text figures that allow readers to visualize a portion of a lesson or example. Visual aids include photographs, maps, charts, illustrations, and graphs.

Read the following excerpt from a math textbook. Draw visual aids in the box below to go with it. Include headings and labels.

A **rectangle** is a four-sided figure with four **right angles.** A **square** is a rectangle with four sides of equal length.

A **triangle** is a three-sided figure. A **right triangle** is a triangle that contains one right angle. The two sides that form the right angle are called **legs.** The third side is called the **hypotenuse.**

Name _____ Date _____

● Vocabulary From the Reading

Use with student book page 48.

> **Key Vocabulary**
>
> evolve   stroll
> jazz   trek
> slim   vast

A. Match each word to its definition.

Example: ___*e*___ slim

1. _____ trek
2. _____ jazz
3. _____ evolve
4. _____ stroll
5. _____ vast

a. to walk slowly
b. to change over time
c. a long and difficult journey
d. very big, wide in area
e. ~~very thin~~
f. a type of American music that emerged in the 1920s

B. Answer the questions.

1. What is the opposite of **slim**? _____

2. Give an example of a place that is vast. _____

3. Explain the difference between a stroll and a trek. Give an example of when you took a stroll and an example of when you made a trek.

_____

_____

_____

_____

4. Describe one way in which you have **evolved** since you were a small child.

_____

_____

_____

_____

Name _____ Date _____

● Reading Strategy
Read Poetry in Sentences

Use with student book page 49.

> **Reading poetry in sentences** can help you make sense of a poem. Look for the punctuation to see where each sentence ends.

Read the poems and answer the questions.

Poem #1

> What could I see
> if I were a bee,
> buzzing through fields
> to my hive in a tree?
> I'd stop every hour
> to nuzzle a flower
> and make pots of honey
> for you to devour!

Poem #2

> I didn't think you noticed when
> I walked into the room. But then
> You spoke to me, without a glance
> In my direction. "If by chance,"
> You asked, "you'd like a cup of tea,
> "Come over here. Sit next to me."

1. How many lines are there in Poem #1? How many sentences are there?

   _____

   _____

2. How many lines are there in Poem #2? How many sentences are there?

   _____

   _____

3. When you read poem #1, after which words would you pause? Write the words here.

   _____

4. When you read poem #2, after which words would you pause? Write the words here.

   _____

Name _____ Date _____

● Text Genre

Use with student book page 49.

Poetry: Lyric Poems

Lyric Poem	
Characteristic	**Definition**
stanzas	groups of lines that share a subject or a theme
rhythm	a musical beat within a line of poetry
rhyme	words that end with a similar sound

Read the poem by Edgar Allan Poe. Read it once silently, and then read it aloud. Focus on the rhythm as you read. Imagine the lines are the words to a song. Can you find the beat? Try clapping along!

"El Dorado," by Edgar Allan Poe (1809–1849)

Gaily bedight,
A **gallant knight,**
In sunshine and in shadow,
Had journeyed long,
Singing a song,
In search of **El Dorado.**

But he grew old—
This knight so bold—
And **o'er** his heart a shadow
Fell as he found
No spot of ground
That looked like El Dorado.

And, as his strength
Failed him at length,
He met a **pilgrim** shadow—
"Shadow," said he,
"Where can it be—
This land of El Dorado?"

"Over the Mountains
Of the Moon,
Down the Valley of the Shadow,
Ride, boldly ride,"
The **shade** replied—
"If you seek for El Dorado!"

Answer the following questions about the poem.

1. How many stanzas are there in this poem? _____

2. How many sentences does each stanza have? _____

3. List four examples of word pairs that rhyme.

_____ and _____; _____ and _____;

_____ and _____; _____ and _____

Gaily bedight dressed in a festive manner
gallant noble, brave
knight medieval horseman
El Dorado legendary city of gold
o'er short for **over**

pilgrim traveler
shade shadow

56

● **Reading Comprehension**

Use with student book page 53.

A. **Retell the story.** What are the main points that Jennifer Trujillo makes in her poem "The Mosaic of English?"

_____

_____

_____

_____

_____

B. **Write your response.** Comment on Trujillo's message in Stanzas 1 and 17. Have you ever encountered an attitude like the man's in Stanza 1? How did you feel about it?

_____

_____

_____

_____

_____

C. **Assess the reading strategy.** Did reading the lines like regular sentences make the poem easier to comprehend? Explain.

_____

_____

_____

_____

_____

Name _____ Date _____

● Spelling

Use with student book page 53.

Words with the Same Sounds but Different Spellings

The words **there, their,** and **they're** have the same sound. When you write, be sure to use the correct spelling.

Word	Meaning	Example
there	location existence	**There** is the cinema. Let's go **there!** **There** are two cinemas in the city.
their	possessive adjective	My parents took **their** car to the mechanic.
they're	contraction of **they are**	I talked to Padma and Rob. **They're** not going to the game tomorrow.

A.   Read the sentences and circle the correct word.

Examples: It takes about two hours by car to drive ((there) / their / they're).

1. (There / Their / They're) are many words in English from Cantonese.

2. I invited them to the poetry reading, but (there / their / they're) too busy.

3. Arabic gave **algebra, candy**, and **caramel** (there / their / they're) names.

4. I rented two movies, but (there / their / they're) both really boring.

5. Can you match the math symbols with (there / their / they're) meanings?

6. (There / Their / They're) going over (there / their / they're) to pick up (there / their / they're) tickets.

B.   Fill in the blanks with **there, their,** or **they're.**

I have two best friends. **(Example)** _____*Their*_____ names are Samir and Alex.

Whenever I have a problem, (1) _____ always (2) _____ if

I need to talk to them. They call me to talk about (3) _____ problems,

too. Samir's house is near mine, and Alex and I often go (4) _____ for

dinner. Samir's family is really nice, and (5) _____ dinners are always

fantastic! I really like Samir and Alex. (6) _____ my best friends!

● Writing Conventions
Punctuation: Quoting Poetry

Use with student book page 53.

If you are quoting a poem in an essay, put quotation marks around the words that you quote. Put a slash (/) between lines of poetry. Follow the original capitalization and punctuation of the poem. Use quotation marks around the title of a poem. Some very long poems will have titles italicized or underlined.

Quotation from a Poem	The old knight in Edgar Allan Poe's "El Dorado" traveled for a long, long time but found "No spot of ground / That looked like El Dorado."

A. Rewrite this sentence with the correct punctuation and capitalization.

In her poem The Mosaic of English, Jennifer Trujillo complains about the difficulty of English spelling. In Stanza 15, she writes: so many cultures pitched into this mix, it's no wonder the spelling still has some tricks.

_____

_____

_____

B. When you need to quote a line that contains text in quotation marks, use single quotation marks.

Quotation Within a Quotation	"*Minnesota* means 'white water'; *Dakota* is a tribe." —Jennifer Trujillo, "Mosaic of English"

Look for lines of poetry that include text in quotation marks. Choose one example from Trujillo's poem (student book pages 50–52) and one from Poe's poem (workbook page 56). Write two sentences quoting these lines.

1. _____

_____

2. _____

_____

Name _____ Date _____

● Vocabulary Development

Use with student book page 55.

Figurative Language

> **Figurative language** is language that goes beyond the literal meanings of words in order to help the reader see an idea or subject in a new way.
>
> **Personification** gives human traits and abilities to nonhuman things. For example, in "The Mosaic of English," Trujillo personifies the Arabic language: "Arabic even got into the games" (Stanza 9). Usually humans play games, not languages.

A. Find the example of personification in each sentence. Underline the nonhuman object and circle the word or words that give it a human trait.

Example: The <u>smell</u> of the rotten sandwich (attacked) me as I opened the bag.

1. The tip of Jimmy's winter hat drooped lazily over his face.

2. My books stubbornly refused to fit into my backpack.

3. The door groaned as it opened.

4. The teapot sang cheerfully as the water came to a boil.

5. At dawn, the sunflowers awoke and turned their faces upward.

B. Use your imagination to think of a way to personify the following nonhuman things. Write a descriptive phrase or verb.

Example: a rocky cliff   *a strong man, standing tall, protecting the valley*

1. a tree covered in snow   _____

2. the moon shining   _____

3. a leaf falling from a tree   _____

4. my alarm clock   _____

C. Now think of an object in your house or at school, perhaps a food item, an appliance, or a piece of clothing. Write a descriptive sentence that personifies that object.

_____

_____

_____

Name _____ Date _____

● **Grammar**

Use with student book page 56.

Noun-Pronoun Agreement and Simple Past Tense

Subject Pronouns: replace subject nouns	Object Pronouns: replace object nouns	Possessive Pronouns: replace possessive nouns
I	me	mine
you	you	yours
she	her	hers
he	him	his
it	it	its
we	us	ours
they	them	theirs

A. Circle the correct pronoun.

Example: That's Andrew—do you know (he /(him)/ his)?

1. Walid got his paper back, but I didn't get (my / me / mine) and you didn't get (your / you / yours). Manu and Stephen didn't get (theirs / their / they), either.

2. (He / She / I) returned from his trip, but I didn't talk to (he / him / her).

3. Sabina and (me / I / mine) sat there, but nobody talked to (we / ours / us).

4. (You / He / I) are very nice to Valerie and (I / me / we).

B. Replace the underlined phrase with an appropriate pronoun. Use editing marks.

Example: Joaquin and I have a dog, but your dog is much bigger.

           We have a dog, but *yours* is much bigger.

1. Carolina walked home from school yesterday. I saw Carolina on Washington Street.

2. If you wear your baseball shirt, and Jorge wears his baseball shirt, then Megan and I will wear our baseball shirts.

3. I bought the new book yesterday, but I didn't start the new book yet. The new book was on sale.

4. Tim and Margarita are doing homework. I saw Tim and Margarita in the library.

Name _____ Date _____

Use with student book page 57.

Use the past tense to write about events that already happened. Most verbs in the past tense end with **-ed.** If a verb ends in **-e,** add **-d** to create the past tense.

C. Rewrite the sentences in the past tense.

Example: Hassan lives in Algeria. _Hassan lived in Algeria._

1. We like the food. _____

2. They finish the homework. _____

3. I watch a movie. _____

4. Melissa works on her report. _____

5. You arrive at 4:00. _____

6. The boys stop playing basketball at 5:00. _____

7. I try to do my best. _____

8. I pat the big dog's head. _____

9. We empty the trash. _____

10. The children behave very well. _____

D. Write about what you, your friends, and your family did last weekend. Use at least five past tense verbs and at least five pronouns. Choose from the following verbs: **help, wash, watch, cook, walk, study, surf, look, research, play, participate, work, smile, laugh, ask,** and **answer.**

_____

_____

_____

_____

_____

Name _____ Date _____

● Grammar Expansion
Pronouns: Use the Correct Form

Be sure that you always use the correct pronoun form when you have compound subjects, objects, or possessive expressions.

Subject:	**You** and **I** are going to study tonight.
Object:	The teacher explained the grammar to **you** and **me**.
Possessive:	This book is **yours** and **mine**.

Note: Always put **I** or **me** last in a compound subject or object.
Jeremy and I played in the park. (*Not* **I and Jeremy**)

A. Choose the correct pronouns to complete the sentences.

Example: Is this book (you /(yours)/ its)?

1. Sanjay's mother bought milkshakes for you and (he / him / his).

2. Adnan spilled sauce on Maria's shirt and (I / me / mine) when he was serving us.

3. Keiko and (I / me / mine) stumbled while climbing the stairs.

4. You and (she / her / hers) should practice English together.

5. I sometimes practice English with you and (she / her / hers).

6. Between you and (I / me / mine), I can't tell the difference between my recipe and (she / her / hers).

B. Correct the errors in the following sentences.

Example: <u>You</u> ~~Me~~ and ~~you~~ <u>I</u> are good drummers.

1. My father, my brother, and me went fishing this morning.

2. I want to know more about you and he.

3. There is always a big argument in class between Dana and they.

4. Our bikes are broken—can you fix both my and him this afternoon?

5. Oh, look, I can see you and she in the group photo!

6. Susie, you need to share this toy with your brothers— it is yours and they!

7. Him and Uri are going to the store.

8. Is this present for you and I?

Name _____ Date _____

● **Grammar Expansion**

Yes / No Questions and Negative Statements in the Simple Past Tense

Use **did** + the base form of the verb to make **yes / no** questions in the past tense.

Did	Subject	Base Verb	
Did	I she / he / it we / you / they	eat	lunch in the cafeteria today?

Use **did not** + the base form of the verb to make negative statements in the past tense.

Subject	Did Not	Base Verb	
I She / He / It We / You / They	did not	like	the lunch today.

Complete the dialogues in the past tense with the missing words.

Example: ___Did___ they ___go___ home?

Yes, they went home a few minutes ago.

1. _____ your brother _____ you with your homework?

   Yes, he helped me.

2. _____ you finish the exam today?

   No, I _____ _____ _____ it. It was too long!

3. _____ the pizza _____ OK?

   Yes, it tasted great!

4. _____ I _____ something wrong?

   No, you _____ _____ say anything wrong.

5. _____ you _____ well on your history test?

   Yes, thanks. I did very well.

6. _____ Luz _____ the book you gave her?

   No, she _____ like it very much. She thought it was too sad.

Name _____ Date _____

● **Writing Assignment**   *Use with student book page 58.*
   A Poem About Something Important to You

Fill in this chart to help you prepare for writing your poem.

1.	Write at least three pets or objects you may want to write about. Then choose one to use for your poem.
2.	Visualize the object or pet you are writing about. List adjectives to describe its color, shape, texture, and size. Think of some vivid, active verbs to describe sounds, sights, and activities associated with the object. **Example Adjectives:** blue, fluffy, raggedy **Example Verbs:** shuffle, slip, slide
3.	Think about figurative language you could use to describe your pet or object. What human traits does it have? Write some phrases or sentences personifying it. **Example:** My slippers wait patiently next to my bed every morning.
4.	Write some details about the object's history and why it is important. How does it make you feel? **Example:** I feel comforted when I put on my favorite old slippers. My grandmother gave them to me for my birthday five years ago.
5.	If you want to write a rhyming poem, think of some rhyming word pairs. **Example:** morning, warning; slip, trip; day, away

Name _____ Date _____

● Writing Assignment
Use with student book page 59.

Writing Support

> **Grammar: Apostrophes and Possessive Nouns, Adjectives, and Pronouns**
>
> All nouns and pronouns can show **possession,** or ownership. For most nouns, add an apostrophe and an **-s** to show possession.
>
>   my daughter**'s** ring   the ruby**'s** glow   the silver**'s** gleam
>
> Possessive nouns, adjectives, and possessive pronouns can do the same thing.

Possessive Noun	Possessive Adjective	Possessive Pronoun
Is this **Roberto's** room?	Is this **his** room?	No, **his** is across the hall.

A.   Combine the two sentences into one. Use a possessive noun.

Example: Abdul Rahim has a hat. His hat is white.

 Abdul Rahim's hat is white.

1. My mother has new shoes. Her shoes were expensive.

 _____

2. The girl has a dog. The dog barks viciously at everyone.

 _____

3. My parrot has feathers. Its feathers are silvery green.

 _____

4. Mr. O'Connor has hair. His hair is wild and fiery red.

 _____

5. Your neighbor has a house. The house looks old and haunted.

 _____

B.   Write three sentences to tell about the things that belong to people you know. Use at least five possessive nouns.

1. _____

2. _____

3. _____

Name _____   Date _____

● Writing Assignment
Revising Activity

Use with student book page 59.

Read each revision tip. Then rewrite the sentences to make them better.

Revision Tip # 1: Use vivid, interesting nouns, adjectives, and verbs.

First Try	A Better Way to Say It
Example: I walked through the nice place.	I strolled through the green, blossoming woods in springtime.
1. I ran from the big dog.	
2. I took the thing.	
3. The soup was good.	
4. I like my old cup.	

Revision Tip # 2: When writing poetry, try to use figurative language. Use your imagination to make these descriptions more interesting. Think of ways to use personification.

First Try	A Better Way to Say It
Example: The wind blew through the trees.	The wind howled and whistled through the trees.
1. The tire finally lost all its air.	
2. The doorbell rang.	
3. I was scared by my shadow.	

Name _____ Date _____

● Writing Assignment

Use with student book page 59.

Editing Activity

A. Read the poem. Fix the errors in spelling and grammar. Use the editing marks on page 455.

My fathers hat was a sight to see,

On the day we went to Tivoli:

Tattered and torn with a big green stain,

It sheltered his head, he said, from the rain.

Before we left, I stoped him and said,

"What is that old, greasy rag on your head?"

He lifted his head with a certain pride.

"Its my grandfathers grandfathers hat," he replyed.

The people we passed in the street, how they stared!

My father didn't care, but I did.

He looked at me, and I looked at he,

And he smiles and said, 'what a sight are we!'

B. Now that you have fixed the grammar and spelling, there is still a problem with lines two and three in the third stanza. What are they? Offer a suggestion for fixing them.

Line 2: _____

_____

_____

Line 3: _____

_____

_____

Name _____ Date _____

● Vocabulary From the Reading

Use with student book page 76.

> **Key Vocabulary**
> fluid   quarrelsome
> impression   reluctantly
> outshine   slew

A. Match each Key Vocabulary word with its definition.

Example: __c__ fluid

1. _____ impression
2. _____ outshine
3. _____ quarrelsome
4. _____ reluctantly
5. _____ slew

a. hostile, combative, wanting to start an argument
b. large quantity, long series
c. ~~smooth, flowing, graceful~~
d. hesitatingly, not wanting to do something
e. idea, image, perception
f. exceed, surpass, do better than

B. Complete each sentence with a Key Vocabulary word.

Example: The girls wore modest dresses to the wedding. They did not want to
_____outshine_____ the bride.

1. Eddie has a reputation for borrowing money and not paying it back. So, I

   _____ gave him $20 when he asked me.

2. My first _____ of Leila was that she was shy and serious. But now that I know her, I see that she is very funny and talks a lot!

3. Fabio is very _____. It's hard to have a conversation with him without getting angry!

4. The art teacher quickly paints a beautiful bird in watercolor with long,

   _____ strokes of the brush.

5. When I returned home late from school, I was greeted with a

   _____ of questions from my parents.

Name _____   Date _____

● Reading Strategy

Use with student book page 77.

Identify Main Ideas

The **main idea** is the most important idea of a reading. The **supporting** details include information that relates to the main idea and help you **deduce** what it is.

Academic Vocabulary for the Reading Strategy	
Word	**Explanation**
support	to agree with, advocate, or back up with information
deduce	to reach a conclusion by reasoning

Read the paragraph about a boy who visits his uncle's apartment. As you read, deduce what the main idea is. Write it down in the box on the left. Note details that support the main idea. Those will go in the box on the right.

> The first room I saw was the kitchen. It was a disaster. Dirty dishes were stacked almost to the ceiling, and empty take-out containers and paper bags littered the counters. The floor was sticky, and I noticed mousetraps in the corners along the walls. Mama and Papa's kitchen never looked like this! We didn't have a modern kitchen, but it was always sparkling clean even though Mama cooked every day with fresh foods from our garden and the market. I got the impression that Uncle didn't cook much at all, and from what I saw, any cooking he did seemed to involve frying an egg or reheating greasy take-out.

Main ideas:	Supporting details:
_____	_____
_____	_____
_____	_____
_____	_____
_____	_____
_____	_____

ne _____   Date _____

● **Text Genre**
Novel

Use with student book page 78.

Novel	
setting	where and when a story takes place
theme	main message or point that an author wants a reader to take from the story
voice	characteristics of the narrator in a story

Read this expanded excerpt from the novel you saw on page 70 of this book.

1 I was excited about coming to live with Uncle in the city, but when I got to Uncle's apartment, I started to reconsider my impressions of city living.

2 The first room I saw was the kitchen. It was a disaster. Dirty dishes were stacked almost to the ceiling, and empty take-out containers and paper bags littered the counters. The floor was sticky, and I noticed mousetraps in the corners along the walls. Mama and Papa's kitchen never looked like this! We didn't have a modern kitchen, but it was always sparkling clean even though Mama cooked every day with fresh foods from our garden and the market. I got the impression that Uncle didn't cook much at all, and from what I saw, any cooking he did seemed to involve frying an egg or reheating greasy take-out.

3 Uncle didn't seem bothered by the state of his kitchen or by the look of horror on my face. "Hey, kid!" he shouted in his gruff, friendly voice as he walked over to me and threw his burly arm around my shoulders, smiling. "Come on in! Are you hungry? I'll fry you an egg. We're going to have a good time here, you and me!"

Answer the questions.

1. Describe the setting of the story. _____

   _____

2. What does the narrator's voice indicate about his age? His character and attitude? _____

   _____

3. What is the theme of this excerpt? What do you predict will happen later in the story?

   _____

   _____

Name ——————————————————— Date ———————————————

● Reading Comprehension

Use with student book pages 85.

Academic Vocabulary for the Reading Comprehension Questions	
Word	**Explanation**
contrast	to compare two things as a way to show their differences
participate	to take part or have a role in an activity or event

A. **Retell the story.** Retell "Behind the Mountains." First give the main idea. Then list the supporting details.

Main Idea: ——————————————————————————————

Supporting Details: ————————————————————————

————————————————————————————————

————————————————————————————————

————————————————————————————————

————————————————————————————————

————————————————————————————————

B. **Write your response.** Describe your first day in a new school. Did you participate in class or in any school activities? Compare and contrast your experience with Celiane's.

————————————————————————————————

————————————————————————————————

————————————————————————————————

————————————————————————————————

C. **Assess the reading strategy.** Did it help you to look for the important ideas and supporting details in order to deduce the main idea on each page? Explain.

————————————————————————————————

————————————————————————————————

————————————————————————————————

————————————————————————————————

● Literary Element

Use with student book page 85.

Tone

> **Tone** is the author's overall attitude toward the reader or the subject.

Read the statements. Each statement comes from a different story, essay, or other writing. Decide what the author's tone is in each one. Circle the best answer.

Example: The highest wind speed ever recorded was on Mount Washington, New Hampshire, on April 12, 1934. It registered 231 miles per hour, which is three times hurricane force.

    a. kind   c. urgent

    b. angry   (d.) impartial

1. The poor dog, shivering with cold, huddled under a store awning to get out of the rain. When the store manager saw the dog, he brought him inside and gave him some food.

    a. funny   c. angry

    b. informal   d. kind

2. It is necessary that we all do something today to save energy.

    a. kind   c. urgent

    b. angry   d. impartial

3. Costa Rica is a popular tourist destination in Central America, with coasts on both the Atlantic and Pacific Oceans.

    a. impartial   c. kind

    b. urgent   d. funny

4. Every day, Ms. Biddy plastered over the cracks in her antique face with three generous coats of makeup. Then she squeezed into a suit that looked like an old sofa and tiny shoes that made her legs wobble like a newborn hippo's. She marched into class, thinking the stares and whispers were simply evidence of deep admiration from her students.

    a. serious   c. sad

    b. funny   d. formal

Name _____ Date _____

● Vocabulary From the Reading

Use with student book page 86.

> **Key Vocabulary**
>
> arrangement   range
> droplet   vapor
> particle

A. Write the Key Vocabulary word for each definition.

Example: _____*vapor*_____ steam; water in gas form

Word	Definition
1. _____	small bead of water
2. _____	order, placement
3. _____	a very small piece
4. _____	a span; extent; series; variety

B. Complete the sentences. Write a different Key Vocabulary word in each blank.

Example: It was getting hot; I could feel _____*droplets*_____ of sweat forming on my forehead.

1. I don't like the _____ of our seats in class—I sit far away from my best friend, but I sit next to the meanest girl in the school.

2. Our class received a wide _____ of grades from **A+** to **F**.

3. There is a _____ of dirt in my eye, which is very annoying!

4. I put my face near the pot of boiling pasta; I love to feel the warm _____ on my skin.

C. Use the four Key Vocabulary words to write sentences about cleaning your kitchen.

1. _____

2. _____

3. _____

4. _____

Name _____ Date _____

● Reading Strategy
Identify Cause and Effect

Use with student book page 87.

> A **cause** is an event or action that produces a result, or an **effect**.

A. Read the following paragraph about the science of cooking. Look for descriptions of cause and effect.

What makes bread rise? Basic bread is made from flour, yeast, water, and salt. Yeast is a living organism that feeds on sugars. When it eats the natural sugars in the flour, it produces carbon dioxide gas and ethyl alcohol. The carbon dioxide gas forms bubbles and makes the bread rise.

Based on the above paragraph, write the effect caused by each action.

1. Yeast eats sugars: _____

2. Carbon dioxide forms bubbles: _____

B. Find at least two causes and effects in the paragraph below. Write them in the chart that follows.

Why do foods get brown when I fry or roast them, but not when I boil them? Foods contain natural sugars such as fructose, glucose, lactose, and maltose. When sugar cooks and browns, this is known as caramelization. Most sugars need to be heated between 160° and 180°C in order to caramelize. However, water can only reach 100°C before it turns to vapor. So, foods cooked in water don't brown because they don't get hot enough for the sugars to caramelize. Oil and air can both reach much higher temperatures, so caramelization is possible in a frying pan or in the oven.

Cause	Effect
1. _____ _____	1. _____ _____
2. _____ _____	2. _____ _____
3. _____ _____	3. _____ _____
4. _____ _____	4. _____ _____

Name _____   Date _____

● Text Genre

Use with student book page 87.

Informational Text: Science Textbook

Science Textbooks	
vocabulary	a group of words related by subject matter
real-life examples	true experiences from real life that prove a point or provide a model for learning
scientific experiments	tests done to see if something happens or works

Read this excerpt from a science textbook.

A physical change is a change in the physical form of a substance. Examples of physical changes include ice melting or sugar dissolving in water. A chemical change is a much bigger change. It produces a new substance. Examples of chemical changes include burning wood or a rusting nail. Today we are going to demonstrate a chemical change.

The Magic Balloon

Procedure:

1. Find a partner. Put on your safety glasses.

2. Pour the vinegar into the bottle.

3. Hold the end of the balloon open so that your partner can put the baking soda inside.

4. Secure the balloon's opening over the bottle. Be sure to keep the baking soda inside the balloon.

> **What you'll need:**
> ○ safety glasses
> ○ an empty 1 L plastic bottle
> ○ 10 g baking soda
> ○ 75 mL white vinegar
> ○ a balloon

5. Finally, lift the bottom of the balloon up so that the baking soda falls into the bottle. Swish the bottle around a little so the baking soda mixes with the vinegar. Then put the bottle down and stand back!

Answer the questions.

1. Which words or terms in this reading might go in a vocabulary box?

   _____

2. Does the reading provide any real-life examples of the concepts it defines? What are the concepts and what are the examples? _____

   _____

   _____

3. Is there a scientific experiment? What result is it trying to show? _____

   _____

Name _____ Date _____

● Reading Comprehension

Use with student book page 91.

A. **Explain the facts.** What scientific facts does the reading describe?

_____

_____

_____

_____

_____

B. **Write your response.** Did any of the information in the reading surprise you? Explain.

_____

_____

_____

_____

_____

C. **Assess the reading strategy.** Did analyzing causes and effects help you follow the reading? Explain.

_____

_____

_____

_____

Name _____ Date _____

● Spelling

Use with student book page 91.

Regular Past Tense Verbs

Most regular verbs just add **–d** or **–ed** in the past tense (decide**d**, hand**ed**, heat**ed**, stay**ed**, fix**ed**, borrow**ed**). But some change further.

Verb Type	Example	Spelling Rule	Past Tense Example
one syllable, one vowel + one consonant (except **w** and **x**)	stop	double final consonant + **-ed**	sto**pped**
more than one syllable, one vowel + one consonant	happen excel	double final consonant if stress falls on second syllable + **-ed**	happen**ed** excel**led**
consonant + **y**	study try	change **y** to **i** + **-ed**	stud**ied** tr**ied**

A. Circle the correct past tense form.

Example: The man (askked /(asked)) about my vaccination and medical papers.

1. The three men (ploted / plotted) the crime together.

2. The class reluctantly (answered / answerred), "Yes."

3. I (hoped / hopped) to do well on the English exam.

4. Gary (denyed / denied) that he forgot to do his homework.

5. The students (plaied / played) during recess.

6. We (followwed / followed) the woman down the hallway.

B. Write three sentences about things you or someone you know did recently. Use at least three of these verbs in the past tense: **regret, look, fry, allow, open, reply, drop, trip, jog, apply, cry, grin, hop, pop, slip, transmit, rely, listen.**

1. _____

2. _____

3. _____

Name _____ Date _____

● Writing Conventions

Use with student book page 91.

Spelling: Abbreviations of Weights, Measurements, and Temperatures

In scientific texts and recipes, use abbreviations for weights, measurements, and temperatures.

	Metric System		English System	
Length	mm	millimeter(s)	in.	inch(es)
	cm	centimeter(s)	ft.	foot / feet
	m	meter(s)	yd.	yard(s)
	km	kilometer(s)	mi.	mile(s)
Volume	ml or mL	milliliter(s)	tsp.	teaspoon(s)
	cl or cL	centiliter(s)	Tbsp.	tablespoon(s)
	l or L*	liter(s)	c.	cup(s)
			qt.	quart(s)
			gal.	gallon(s)
Weight	g	gram(s)	oz.	ounce(s)
	kg	kilogram(s)	lb. / lbs.	pound / pounds
Temperature	°C	degree(s) Celsius	°F	degree(s) Fahrenheit

* Sometimes it is written in uppercase to distinguish the letter *l* from the number 1.

A. Rewrite the following text using abbreviations. Follow the example.

Example: Add two pounds of potatoes to two gallons of boiling water.

Add 2 lbs. potatoes to 2 gal. boiling water.

1. You will need one liter of water and five grams of salt.

   _____

2. Water boils at 100 degrees Celsius and 212 degrees Fahrenheit.

   _____

3. Use a piece of wood three feet long and six inches wide.

   _____

4. Mix two cups of flour, one cup of milk, two eggs, and one teaspoon of salt.

   _____

B. Write two instructions for a recipe or science experiment. Use abbreviations.

1. _____

2. _____

Name _____ Date _____

● Vocabulary Development
Words with Multiple Meanings

Use with student book page 93.

Some words have more than one meaning. Use the context of a word to understand which meaning is being used.

Read the words and their definitions.

> **fluid 1** *n.* liquid **2** *adj.* smooth, flowing, graceful
> **matter 1** *n.* subject or topic **2** *n.* material in the universe that has mass and volume **3** *v.* to be important
> **period 1** *n.* a length of time **2** *n.* a session in the academic day **3** *n.* a specific era or time in history **4** *n.* punctuation at the end of a sentence in the form of a dot (.)
> **record 1** *v.* to write down **2** *v.* to register sound or video on tape, CD, or DVD **3** *n.* an official document or written information **4** *n.* a collection of known facts about someone **5** *n.* (in sports) the highest or best level reached
> **rose 1** *n.* a type of flower **2** *v.* past tense of **rise**
> **row 1** *n.* a line or orderly arrangement **2** *n.* a quarrel, argument **3** *v.* to move a boat forward using oars

A. Decide which definition of each underlined word is being used. Write the number on the line.

Example: ___1___ When you have a cold, you should drink plenty of <u>fluids</u>.

1. _____ After each scientific experiment, you should <u>record</u> your results.

2. _____ We can go home today after fourth <u>period</u>.

3. _____ Manuel gave Celia a <u>rose</u> for Valentine's Day.

4. _____; _____; _____ The Haitian girl in the third <u>row</u> <u>rose</u> to give her opinion on the <u>matter</u>.

5. _____; _____ We can <u>row</u> to shore or use the motor. It doesn't <u>matter</u> to me.

B. Choose two of the words from the list above. Write two sentences for each word. In each sentence, use a different meaning of the word.

1. _____

2. _____

3. _____

4. _____

Milestones C • Copyright © Heinle

Name _____ Date _____

● Grammar
The Present Progressive Tense

Use with student book page 94.

Use the present progressive tense to describe an action that is happening now.

Present Progressive Tense		
subject	*be*	verb + *-ing*
I	am	driving.
You / We / They	are	studying.
He / She / It	is	singing.

A. Write sentences in the present progressive tense using the clues. Add details to make the sentence more interesting.

Example: Arturo / eat _Arturo is eating a salad._____

1. Rolf and Helene / read

   _____

2. I / listen

   _____

3. Anna and I / study

   _____

4. the dog / play

   _____

5. you / practice

   _____

B. Write five sentences about what you are doing and what is happening right now where you are.

1. _____

2. _____

3. _____

4. _____

5. _____

Name _____   Date _____

● Grammar

Use with student book page 95.

The Past Progressive Tense

The past progressive **tense** describes actions that were in progress at some point in the past. Sometimes this tense indicates actions that were interrupted.

Past Progressive Tense		
subject	*be*	verb + *-ing*
I	was	driving.
You / We / They	were	studying.
He / She / It	was	singing.

A. Complete the statements with the correct form of the past progressive.

Example: Horacio _____was playing_____ (play) video games while I ate lunch.

1. My father _____ (shave) when I knocked on the door.

2. I _____ (dream) when the alarm clock went off this morning.

3. I don't know what Sergio _____ (think) when he bought Marcella that ugly hat!

4. The kids _____ (put) on their jackets in the kitchen when they saw the school bus drive by the house.

5. We _____ (wait) for a long time in the doctor's office before anyone came out to see us.

B. What was everyone doing? Write five sentences about what was happening in your home last night at 9:00.

1. _____

2. _____

3. _____

4. _____

5. _____

Milestones C • Copyright © Heinle

Name _____ Date _____

● Grammar Expansion

Present Progressive Tense for Planned Activities in the Future

Sometimes you can use the present progressive tense to describe events that are planned for the future.

> I **am traveling** to Spain next winter with my family.
> What **are you doing** tonight?
> Our class **is having** a party next Friday.

A. Check off the sentences that describe future events.

1. _____ We are getting out of school early this afternoon.

2. _____ We are learning about the Civil War in our history class now.

3. _____ My sister is getting dressed, so we should wait for her.

4. _____ You are coming to our house for dinner tonight, right?

B. Change the following sentences to the present progressive tense to express the same idea.

Example: My friends are going to go horseback riding tomorrow.
    My friends are going horseback riding tomorrow.

1. My mother and I are going to bake a cake tonight.

   _____

2. My father is going to travel to Belgium next month.

   _____

3. Our class is going to perform a play for the school next week.

   _____

4. You are going to help me with my homework later!

   _____

C. Use the present progressive to write about things that you plan to do.

1. _____

2. _____

3. _____

4. _____

Name _____ Date _____

● Grammar Expansion

Yes / No Questions and Negative Statements in the Present and Past Progressive Tenses

Questions in the Present Progressive Tense		
Question	Am	I	
	Is	he / she / it	speaking to Laura?
	Are	we / you / they	

Negative Answers in the Present Progressive Tense		
Answer	I	am not	
	He / She / It	is not	speaking to Laura?
	We / You / They	are not	

Questions in the Past Progressive Tense		
Question	Was	I / he / she / it	dreaming?
	Were	we / you / they	

Negative Answers in the Past Progressive Tense		
Answer	I / He / She / It	was not	dreaming.
	We / You / They	were not	

Fill in the missing questions in the dialogue.

Example: _Was Dad singing in the shower this morning?_
Yes, he was singing in the shower this morning.

1. _____
   No, I was not snoring during class.

2. _____
   Yes, we are going with you to the play.

3. _____
   No, he is not coming to the party.

4. _____
   Yes, she was doing homework last night at 8:00.

84

Name ——————————————————————— Date ————————————————

● Writing Assignment
Descriptive Essay

Use with student book pages 96–97.

A. Brainstorm a list of details from the painting *Sandía/Watermelon*. In the left column, list people and things you see in the painting. On the right, write phrases that describe them, what they are doing, or what is happening around them.

Detail	Description
Grandmother	barefoot, sitting on the porch swing

B. Look over your list of details and descriptions. Decide what the main idea in the painting is. Write your thesis statement based on this idea.

Main Idea	Thesis Statement

Name _____ Date _____

● Writing Assignment
Writing Support

Use with student book page 97.

Mechanics: Hyphens and Dashes

Hyphens are used in three ways.
- In numbers (twenty-one) and fractions used as adjectives (two-thirds vote)
- With the prefixes **ex-, pro-, self-,** and **anti-** (ex-partner, pro-recycling, self-starter, anti-slavery)
- In compound adjectives before a noun they modify (after-school meeting, well-planned party)

Dashes are used to indicate a break in thought.
  The game was delayed for three days—the playing fields were too muddy for use.
  Mother planted cosmos—bright pink and purple flowers—in her flower bed.

A. Read each statement and decide whether the two underlined words should be separated by a hyphen or a dash. Write **H** for hyphen or **D** for dash.

Example: __H__ This Web based computer program is exactly what we need.

1. _____ The candidate supports strong anti pollution policies.

2. _____ In art class we are making environment related collages.

3. _____ We are making our collages using words and pictures we cut out from magazines we are using mostly nature and science magazines.

4. _____ On Earth Day it is coming up soon, soon our collages will hang near the entrance of the school.

B. Rewrite these sentences. Add hyphens or dashes where necessary.

1. Mr. Fleischer has a well adjusted relationship with his ex wife.

_____

2. The movie we saw an action film was a two hour waste of money.

_____

3. I loved the self help book you gave me I read it all in one afternoon.

_____

4. My new shirt a blue cotton blouse has three quarter sleeves.

_____

Milestones C • Copyright © Heinle

Name _____ Date _____

● **Writing Assignment**   *Use with student book page 97.*
Revising Activity

Look at this paragraph about a painting. It has some sentences that don't fit.

(1) Van Gogh uses warm colors to show a cozy, inviting scene in his *Café Terrace at Night*. (2) It hangs in the Kröller-Müller Museum in Otterlo, Netherlands. (3) The terrace—or patio—of the café is lit with a bright lamp, which bathes everything around it in cheerful yellow and orange. (4) A waiter serves several customers, who sit and socialize at bright, white tabletops. (5) The café was in Arles, where he was living at the time. (6) Arles is a small city in the south of France. (7) The sky is a vivid blue filled with large, luminous stars. (8) Warm orange lights glow in the windows of the apartments across the street. (9) Van Gogh used a lot of bright yellows and blues in many of his paintings. (10) Even the cobblestones on the street are tinted with white, yellow, violet, and pink. (11) People dressed in yellow, red, and lime green stroll by, surely on the way to—or from—some pleasant activity!

Now answer the following questions.

1. Which sentence represents the main idea, or thesis statement?

   _____

2. Which sentences provide supporting details? _____

   _____

3. Which sentences do *not* support the thesis statement? _____

   _____

4. The paragraph is missing a conclusion. Which of the following sentences would make the best conclusion?

   a. Van Gogh was so excited about this painting that he wrote his sister a letter about it.

   b. Van Gogh painted this scene at night, so he was not always sure about the exact shade of color he was using.

   c. In this painting, Van Gogh wants to show that nighttime scenes don't have to be dull and dark—there are also glowing lights and beautiful colors to see at night.

   d. The café still exists—now as the Café Van Gogh—and the exterior is painted in the same colors—yellow and green—that Van Gogh painted it in the *Café Terrace*.

87

Name _____   Date _____

● Writing Assignment
Editing Activity

Use with student book page 97.

Read this composition and mark the mistakes using the editing marks on page 455. Look for missing hyphens and dashes, incorrect spelling of present participles, and incorrect use of the present and past progressive tenses. Then rewrite the paragraphs correctly.

1 James McNeill Whistler was an important nineteenth century American born artist. He lived most of his life in London and Paris. His most famous painting is probably *Arrangement in Grey and Black: The Artist's Mother* a portrait most people now call *Whistler's Mother*. Whistler and his mother are living in London when he painted it in 1861.

2 In the painting, Whistler's mother is siting in a chair faceing left and lookking straight ahead. She has a serious expression on her face. She is wear all black except for a white bonnet on her head. To her left, there is a painting actually an earlier painting by Whistler himself hanging on the grey wall.

_____

_____

_____

_____

_____

_____

_____

_____

_____

_____

_____

_____

_____

Name _____ Date _____

● Vocabulary From the Reading

Use with student book page 102.

> **Key Vocabulary**
>
> crisis   framework
> debt   impose
> enforce   resolve

A. Write the correct the Key Vocabulary word next to its definition.

Example: ____framework____ basis; structure; foundation

1._____	an emergency situation
2._____	put upon; force upon
3._____	something owed to someone else, such as money
4._____	fix (a problem)
5._____	carry out; ensure obedience to (a law or rule)

B. Choose the correct Key Vocabulary word to complete each sentence.

Example: __b__ How are we going to _____ this problem?

     a. enforce   b. resolve   c. impose

1. _____ Thank you for all your help. I am in your _____.

     a. framework   b. crisis   c. debt

2. _____ To strengthen his power, the king _____ a slew of new laws on his people.

     a. imposed   b. resolved   c. enforced

3. _____ Our police officers are here to _____ the laws.

     a. resolve   b. enforce   c. impose

C. Using three Key Vocabulary words, write a paragraph about a crisis you resolved.

_____

_____

_____

Name _____ Date _____

● Reading Strategy

Use with student book page 103.

Organize Information

> **Organizing information** into an outline can help you understand more of what you read by **sequencing** events and understanding the **influences** that are important in the reading.

Academic Vocabulary for the Reading Strategy	
Word	**Explanation**
sequence	a connected series of events or items, one following the other
influence	to change someone's mind or have an effect on

Read the paragraph about the U.S. flag.

During its first year of independence, the newly formed United States passed through many unofficial flag designs, including several depicting a rattlesnake and one depicting a miniature Union Jack—the British flag—in the upper left corner with 13 red and white stripes representing the 13 original colonies. But on June 14, 1777, Congress acted to establish the first official flag of the newly formed nation. They kept the 13 red and white stripes, but they replaced the British symbol with 13 white stars on a blue background to represent the formation of "a new constellation." Since its adoption as the official flag, the Stars and Stripes hasn't changed all that much in its basic design. Today, the number of stars has increased to 50, representing the 50 states in the union, and the flag still retains the 13 original stripes, largely because the addition of extra stripes became impractical once the union passed 15 states.

Fill in the outline with the key information from the paragraph. Make sure the information appears in the correct sequence. The main idea should follow the Roman numeral **I**.

I. _____

    A. _____

        1. _____

        2. _____

    B. _____

        1. _____

        2. _____

Name _____ Date _____

● Text Genre
Informational Text: Magazine Article

Use with student book page 104.

Magazine Article: History	
dates	important days, months, and years
events	specific important happenings
chronological order	order in which events take place

Read the passage from a historical article.

The American Revolution, in Brief

1 Tension between the American colonies and Britain rose in the 1760s, when Britain began imposing heavy taxes on the colonists. The colonists had no representatives in British Parliament, so they were very angry. In 1765, Britain passed the Stamp Act, a tax to pay for military services, but the colonists protested so violently, it was impossible to enforce and was quickly repealed. Others followed and were also met with protest. The British sent troops to the colonies to enforce their laws in 1768. The Americans greatly resented their presence. In 1773, a group of Bostonians snuck onto a British ship at night and dumped crates of tea into Boston Harbor in protest of a tea tax. This incident became known as the "Boston Tea Party."

2 The first shots of the American Revolution were fired in 1775 at Lexington and Concord, Massachusetts. The following year, the Declaration of Independence was ratified by Congress in Philadelphia, but the Revolution was not over yet. In 1778, France agreed to help the Americans in the war, and in 1781 the French and the Americans defeated British troops in an important battle at Yorktown, Virginia. Britain and the United States signed a peace treaty in 1783.

A time line is a chronology of events. Fill in the time line below with the missing dates or events from the passage above.

1. _____ _____ 1765	British send troops 2. _____	3. _____ _____ 1773	4. _____ _____ 1775

Declaration of Independence 5. _____	6. _____ _____ 1778	7. _____ _____ 1781	Peace treaty, England & U.S. 8. _____

Name _____ Date _____

● Reading Comprehension

Use with student book page 111.

Academic Vocabulary for the Reading Comprehension Questions	
Word	Explanation
solution	an answer to a problem, or a way to solve a problem
trigger	to cause something to start; start a reaction

A. **Retell the story.** Review your outline for "Crisis of Government." Choose the five most important events and write them in the correct sequence below. Be sure to include the events that triggered the crisis as well as the leaders' solution.

_____

_____

_____

_____

_____

B. **Write your response.** Do you think Shays's rebellion was justified? Why?

_____

_____

_____

_____

_____

C. **Assess the reading strategy.** How does organizing information in an outline help you understand the reading?

_____

_____

_____

_____

Name _____ Date _____

● Text Element

Audience

Use with student book page 111.

> An author writes for an **audience**—the readers who are going to read the work.

A. Read each title of a magazine article. Then identify the audience that the author has in mind.

Example: ___a___ "You Don't Need TV! Five Cool Games to Play on a Rainy Day"

1. _____ "SuperSonic Video Device: Easy to Use and a Lot of Fun!"

2. _____ "Final Exams: A Survival Guide"

3. _____ "Micro-Revolution: Will Sato, Inc.'s New 500 Gigabyte Solar-Powered Microcomputer Take the Country by Storm?"

4. _____ "Ten Things Every Mother Should Tell Her Daughter"

5. _____ "Tunisia: A Mosaic of History and Culture"

a. ~~children~~

b. people who like to travel

c. women

d. students

e. technology experts

f. people who are interested in technology but don't know much about it

B. Describe what kind of article might appeal to each of the following audiences.

Example: Scientists: *An article about new discoveries about Mercury*

1. Immigrant kids: _____

2. Sports fans: _____

3. People interested in art: _____

4. People who like to read books: _____

5. Teachers: _____

6. People who like to cook: _____

7. Pet lovers: _____

Name _____ Date _____

● Vocabulary From the Reading

Use with student book page 112.

> **Key Vocabulary**
>
> audition   monologue
> enunciate   panel

A. Write the Key Vocabulary word for each definition.

Word	Definition
Example: _____*panel*_____	a group of people called to serve on a project, in a discussion, or as judges
1. _____	a speech; a scene or performance in which one actor speaks to himself or to the audience
2. _____	to try out for a role in the performing arts; a performance with the goal of getting a role
3. _____	to speak clearly

B. Use one of the Key Vocabulary words to complete each statement.

Example: I have a singing _____*audition*_____ this afternoon for a part in the school chorus.

1. I can't understand a word you're saying. You need to _____!

2. The stand-up comedian's _____ was funny last night.

3. The radio host invited a _____ of experts to discuss the matter on his program.

4. The actress is practicing her lines for an _____ tomorrow.

C. Write sentences about situations in your own life. Use a Key Vocabulary word in each sentence.

1. _____

2. _____

3. _____

Name _____   Date _____

● **Reading Strategy**   *Use with student book page 113.*
Make and Revise Predictions

> When you predict, you guess what will happen in the future based on clues in the
> past or in the present. You **revise predictions** by changing your guess based on
> new information.

A. Read Paragraph 1 and make a prediction based on clues in the story. Fill in the
chart.

I felt really weird and nervous on my first day at the new school. It was
very different from my old school, and I didn't know anyone. When I walked
into my homeroom, I could tell I was going to have problems. Everyone stared
at me, and no one smiled. Some tough-looking kids in the back whispered to
each other and laughed. I sat in the only empty seat and drew pictures in my
notebook. The rest of my classes went pretty much the same way. The kids who
didn't ignore me just said mean things to me, especially Bobby Perkins, who
was unfortunately in all my classes.

Clues in the Story	Prediction

B. Read Paragraph 2 and revise your prediction based on new information in the
story.

To amuse myself, I started drawing pictures of the teachers and kids in my
class. I drew whole comic strips where each student in the class had a role.
Some of the kids sitting near me saw it and thought it was hilarious. When
Bobby Perkins saw it, he was pretty angry because he had a very negative role
in the comic strip. He took the page and ripped it up. I thought it was funny
that he acted that way. He was acting just like his character in the comic strip!
So, the next day I produced another comic strip making fun of the incident.
Everyone else in the class loved it so much that a student who worked on the
school newspaper asked if I would draw a regular comic for the paper. Bobby
looked horrified, so I sent him a secret note telling him not to worry. I would not
humiliate him in the school paper if he agreed to be nice to me!

New Information	Revised Prediction

Name _____ Date _____

● **Text Genre**   *Use with student book page 113.*

Memoir

Memoir	
first-person point of view	told by a narrator who is one of the characters in the story; the narrator uses the pronoun "I"
dialogue	conversation between characters
internal dialogue	thoughts of the narrator, revealed for the reader

Read the following excerpt from a memoir.

1 "Amanda Bates," called a stern voice from the front of the room.

2 "That's you, sweetie," whispered Mom, jabbing me with her elbow. "Go on! Good luck!"

3 "OK," I whispered back. Then I rose to my feet and walked shakily to the front of the silent conference room. It was my turn to perform. I sat down in the folding chair and pressed my clarinet to my dry lips, droplets of sweat forming on my forehead. A panel of judges sat facing me—four serious women in suits looking at me expectantly. Behind me, I could feel the eyes of all the anxious parents and fellow competitors burning into my back. Most of them were eagerly waiting for my first mistake while my parents were hoping for a perfect performance. I blew the first note—a horrible squeak! I started again. My eyes were closed as I tried to remember the notes from the four-page classical piece I had memorized, but I could feel everyone else's eyes wide-open in front of me and behind me, all of them looking at me, waiting. The notes began dancing around in my head, crazy notes dancing everywhere… Oh, what was I playing? I could feel the music slipping out of my control. What would my parents say?

Answer the questions.

1. Is this story told from a first-person point of view? Give an example from the

   text. Who is the narrator? _____

   _____

2. Is there dialogue in the story? Between which characters? _____

   _____

3. Give an example of internal dialogue from the story. _____

   _____

4. How is the character feeling? How do you know? _____

   _____

● **Reading Comprehension**   *Use with student book page 119.*

A. **Retell the story.** Summarize the main points from the reading "A Shot at It."

_____

_____

_____

_____

B. **Write your response.** Did you ever have to speak or perform in front of an audience or panel? Give details. How did you feel?

_____

_____

_____

_____

_____

C. **Assess the reading strategy.** How can making and revising predictions help you understand a reading?

_____

_____

_____

_____

Name _____ Date _____

● Spelling

Use with student book page 119.

Possessive Nouns Ending in -s

When a name ends in **-s**, add **'s** to make it possessive, like you do with any other noun.	Shays's rebellion
When a singular noun ends in **-s**, add **'s**	the dress's sleeves
For plural nouns ending in **-s**, just add an apostrophe (').	individuals' and states' rights

A. Circle the correct possessive noun.

Example: My (parents's /(parents')) car is very old.

1. The (bus' / bus's) lights were flashing, so we had to stop the car.

2. The (boys' / boys's) baseball team is holding tryouts tomorrow.

3. The (princess' / princess's) hair was very, very long.

4. Mrs. (Adams' / Adams's) husband is running for Congress.

5. Our (neighbors' / neighbors's) dog is very vicious.

6. The (birds' / birds's) nest is right above our back porch.

B. Add an apostrophe or an apostrophe + **s** to make the nouns possessive.

Example: My dog __'s__ belly never fills!

1. Mr. Marius ____ class is my favorite.

2. The class ____ seating arrangement is posted at the front of the room.

3. Many countries ____ first or second language is French.

4. Celiane is in the the ladies ____ room.

5. The writers of the Articles of Confederation tried to protect states ____ rights.

6. Congress ____ power was limited by the Articles of Confederation.

7. Carlos ____ parents go to all of his soccer games.

8. The babies ____ toys are all over the floor.

9. My father ____ job is very difficult.

10. The school bus ____ seats are very uncomfortable.

Name _____ Date _____

● Writing Conventions
Spelling: Heteronyms

Use with student book page 119.

Heteronyms are words that are spelled the same but are pronounced differently. Each pronunciation has a different meaning.

Word 1	Meaning	Word 2	Meaning
minute (n.) min´it	60 seconds	**minute** (adj.) mī nüt´	tiny, very small
protest (n.) prō´test	public show of objection	**protest** (v.) prə test´	to object
address (n.) ad´res	place of residence	**address** (v.) ə dres´	to speak directly to (someone)
house (n.) hous	home, dwelling	**house** (v.) houz	to give a place to live
lead (n.) led	a heavy metal	**lead** (v.) lēd	to guide
close (adj.) klōs	near	**close** (v.) klōz	to shut (opposite of **open**)
content (n.) kon´tent	something contained; material in a text	**content** (adj.) kən tent´	satisfied; happy
object (n.) ob´jekt	an item, a thing	**object** (v.) əb jekt´	to oppose; to disagree
project (n.) proj´ekt	a task	**project** (v.) prə jekt´	to send forward

Write the part of speech of the word in bold. If it has two syllables, make an accent mark (') to show which sound is emphasized. Then read the sentence aloud with the correct pronunciation.

Example: The child has a **minúte** fracture in her leg. ____*adjective*____

1. Stephanie, could you come here for a **minute**? _____

2. I'm working on an important science **project**. _____

3. The store is going to **close** in ten minutes. _____

4. These apartment buildings **house** over 1,000 people. _____

5. Cats close their eyes and purr when they feel **content**. _____

6. Do you live **close** to the school? _____

7. The principal will **address** the students at the assembly. _____

8. I found a strange **object** on the sidewalk yesterday. _____

9. Will you **protest** if I turn off the radio? _____

10. Water containing **lead** is dangerous to drink. _____

Milestones C • Copyright © Heinle

Name _____ Date _____

● Vocabulary Development

Use with student book page 121.

Prefix: fore-

A **prefix** is a word part, or a group of letters, added to the beginning of a word to change the word's meaning. The prefix **fore-** means "before" or "in front of."

A. Predict the definition of each underlined word. Write your predictions on the lines.

1. The horse's <u>forelegs</u> are very strong.

   Prediction: _____

2. The weather <u>forecast</u> calls for rain and thunderstorms.

   Prediction: _____

3. Dr. Ikeda is the <u>foremost</u> expert on nutrition in the hospital.

   Prediction: _____

4. The dog bit my <u>forearm</u> when I tried to push him away.

   Prediction: _____

5. The surprise party we threw for our friend required a lot of <u>forethought</u>.

   Prediction: _____

B. Now look the words up in a dictionary. Were your predictions correct?

1. Definition of **forelegs:** _____

2. Definition of **forecast:** _____

3. Definition of **foremost:** _____

4. Definition of **forearm:** _____

5. Definition of **forethought:** _____

C. Use the words **forefathers, foresee,** and **forethought** in a paragraph about your life or family history.

_____

_____

_____

Name _____ Date _____

● Grammar

Use with student book page 122.

Adjectives and Adverbs

Adjectives modify, or describe, nouns. An adjective can describe a noun by telling about the quality or quantity of the noun.

A **predicate adjective** is separated from the noun it modifies by a linking verb.

adjective   predicate adjective

The **green** apple looks **ripe**.

An **adverb** is a word used to describe a verb, an adjective, or another adverb. An adverb can describe by telling how, when, where, or to what extent (how much).

Adverb	What it Modifies	What it Tells
She walks **everywhere**.	verb: walks	where she walks (**everywhere**)
She is an **extremely** fast walker.	adjective: fast	how she walks (**extremely** fast)
She walks **very** slowly.	adverb: slowly	how much (how slowly) she walks (**very** slowly)

A. Circle the adjectives. Underline the adverbs.

1. Jennifer is an incredibly sweet girl.

2. The Cuban student dances very skillfully.

3. Stephen is an unusually handsome young man.

4. The tall boys with the dark brown hair are twin brothers.

5. The sixth-grade class is going somewhere with their English teacher.

B. Rewrite these sentences. Add at least one adjective and adverb to each sentence.

1. I read the book. _____.

2. The student speaks. _____.

3. My friends laugh. _____.

4. We ate the food. _____.

5. I walked through the snow. _____.

Name _____ Date _____

● Grammar

Use with student book page 123.

Adjective and Adverb Phrases

Adjective phrases are used in the same way as adjectives—to modify a noun. An adjective phrase is a group of words that indicates what kind or which one. The phrase usually begins with a preposition such as **in, by, near, with, about, on, over, from, before,** and **down,** and ends with a noun.

> The fireplace provided warmth **from the bitter cold.**
> (what kind of warmth)

Adverb phrases work like adverbs—to modify verbs by telling how, when, where, to what extent, and why. They also begin with a preposition and end with a noun.

> She rehearses **with determination.**
> (how she rehearses)

A. Underline the adjective or adverb phrases in each sentence. Circle the modified word. Label each phrase **adjective** or **adverb.** Draw an arrow from the label to the phrase.

Example: She (auditioned) at the Performing Arts school. _____Adverb_____

1. The bread on the table is fresh and warm. _____

2. Charlie put the pie in the refrigerator. _____

3. Martina often goes with her sister to the mall. _____

4. The boy with the round glasses sits at the cafeteria table. _____

5. Students at the arts school learn correct enunciation. _____

B. Add an adjective or adverb phrase to each of the following sentences. After the sentence, say which type of phrase you added.

Example: The girl <u>from Idaho</u> is very friendly. _____adjective phrase_____

1. I do my homework _____. _____

2. The food _____ is good. _____

3. The store _____ is not expensive. _____

4. The movie _____ was interesting. _____

5. My friends usually go _____. _____

Name _____ Date _____

● Grammar Expansion
Nouns as Adjectives

> Sometimes nouns can act as adjectives when they modify other nouns.
> > a pizza with cheese → a cheese pizza
> > an instructor of dance → a dance instructor
> The noun acting as an adjective is usually singular.
> > a bag for books → a book bag

A. In the following sentences, circle the nouns acting as adjectives.

Example: My mother has a nice (leather) bag.

1. The dancer took off her ballet slippers and put on some cotton socks.

2. Aunt Mayda's noodle casserole was a hit at the family dinner.

3. I cleaned the bird cages with an old bath towel.

4. She broke her coffee cup, so she drank out of a soup bowl.

B. Replace the underlined phrases with a noun acting as an adjective to modify another noun.

Example: There's a new soap for hands in the bathroom.
>   There's a new hand soap in the bathroom.

1. I left my book about science at school.

   _____

2. I ate a sandwich of ham for lunch.

   _____

3. If you have a card for the library, you can take books home.

   _____

4. We had to take our dog to the hospital for animals last night.

   _____

5. Our visit to the museum was very interesting.

   _____

6. Ousmane has a very large collection of coins.

   _____

● Grammar Expansion

Adverbs of Frequency

Use these adverbs to talk about how often an action happens. They are listed from least frequent to most frequent:

never	sometimes
almost never	often, frequently
rarely	almost always
occasionally	always, all the time, every day

Placement
Place the adverbs between the subject and the verb, except for **all the time** and **every day**, which go at the end of the sentence: I **never** go to the mall. I go to the park **all the time.**
Occasionally, sometimes, often, and **every day** can also go at the beginning or end of the sentence: **Occasionally,** I go to the movies. I go to my aunt's house **sometimes.**

A.   Rewrite the sentences. Correct the errors in the underlined phrases.

Example: Aimee loves French food. Rarely she eats it.

She often eats it.

1.   Samira hates sports. Frequently she goes to soccer games.

_____

2.   I love Italian food. I all the time eat in Italian restaurants.

_____

3.   Never we go outside during a snowstorm. We are afraid!

_____

4.   Viktor likes horror movies. He watches rarely them.

_____

B.   Answer the questions. Give true answers about yourself in complete sentences. Use adverbs of frequency.

1.   Do you ever go to the movies? _____

2.   How often do you read books for fun? _____

_____

Milestones C • Copyright © Heinle

Name _____ Date _____

● **Writing Assignment**   *Use with student book pages 124–125.*
Expository Essay about a Problem and a Solution

Complete this page to help you organize your thoughts before you write your three-paragraph essay.

Choose a problem and brainstorm possible solutions. Circle the best solution.

Problem: _____

Solutions: _____

_____

_____

Use the library to research information on the problem and solution you chose. Make a three-paragraph outline in the space below to organize the information you find.

I. Introduction __A.__ _____

_____

_____

_____

_____

II. Body _____

_____

_____

_____

_____

III. Conclusion _____

_____

_____

_____

_____

Name _____   Date _____

● Writing Assignment

Use with student book page 125.

Writing Support

> **Grammar: Comparative and Superlative Adjectives and Adverbs**
> Adjectives and adverbs that compare a degree of quality are called positives, comparatives, and superlatives.

Positive	Comparative	Superlative
big	bigg**er**	bigg**est**
young	young**er**	young**est**
cheaply	**more** cheaply	**most** cheaply
happy	happ**ier**	happ**iest**
bad	**worse**	**worst**

A.   Fill in the correct comparative or superlative form of the positive adjective.

Example: (big) In my opinion, the _____ *biggest* _____ problem in the world today is pollution of the environment.

1. (dirty) The air is _____ than it was 100 years ago.

2. (rich) The United States is one of the _____ countries in the world.

3. (bad) Some people's living conditions are _____ than others'.

4. (poorly) In general, students at that school score _____ in math and science than students at other schools.

5. (sad) Everyone was sad, but I was probably the _____ of all!

B.   Write five sentences about your community or neighborhood using comparative and superlative adjectives and adverbs.

1. _____

2. _____

3. _____

4. _____

5. _____

Milestones C • Copyright © Heinle

Name _____ Date _____

● Writing Assignment
Revising Activity

Use with student book page 125.

Practice these Revision Tips to help you refine your writing.

A. Revision Tip # 1: Consider your audience and your tone. This is a formal essay about a problem and a solution. Avoid informal language and too much reference to yourself.

First Try	A Better Way to Say It
Example: It would be so cool if all the bikers in the community listened to me and started wearing their helmets!	Our community would be much safer if all bikers remembered to wear their helmets.
1. I think the food in the cafeteria is so gross. I don't know how anyone eats there every day!	
2. We're all going to be obese if we don't stop sitting around watching TV and start playing outside!	
3. I love art and music so much. I think it's so sad that a lot of schools are cutting these programs.	

B. Revision Tip # 2: Back up your opinions with evidence. It's OK to say what you think, but you need to show why your opinion is valid.

First Try	A Better Way to Say It
Example: I think my solution is the best. I just know it will work!	I believe this will be the best solution for the community based on the experiences of my own family.
1. People who ride bikes should wear helmets. It's that simple!	
2. I think drinking soda is bad. We should drink water.	
3. People our age should do volunteer work.	

Name _____ Date _____

● Writing Assignment

Use with student book page 125.

Editing Activity

A. Read this essay. Mark the mistakes using the editing marks on page 455.

A Very Heavy Problem

    Mrs. Nackiss moved into an old house in our neighborhood with hers husband and two little daughters two years ago. Unfortunately, she heard never about lead poisoning, so she didnt check the house for lead paint, one of the baddest hidden household dangers! Lead is a toxic heavily metal, and it is dangerously because it can cause developmental damage in children if ingested. Sure enough, not long after they moved in, Mrs. Nackiss' younger daughter was diagnosed with mild lead poisoning. The girl received treatment immediate. Then the family had to remove the lead from theirs house. It was'nt cheap to do this, but for Mrs. Nackiss, her daughters's health was the more important thing in the world. Now Mrs. Nackiss want's to educate the community about this problem.

B. Rewrite the essay correctly.

_____

_____

_____

_____

_____

_____

_____

_____

_____

_____

_____

Name _____ Date _____

● Vocabulary From the Reading

Use with student book page 142.

> **Key Vocabulary**
>
> depressed   ignorant
> embarrassed   obvious
> graduate   old-fashioned

A. Circle the correct Key Vocabulary word in each sentence.

Example: I hope we all ((graduate)/ ignorant) at the end of high school.

1. Linda's ideas are (obvious / old-fashioned). She sounds like my grandmother!

2. Those kids are so (depressed / ignorant). They don't understand anything about other cultures!

3. The test was really easy. The answers were so (old-fashioned / obvious)!

4. My friend was really (embarrassed / depressed) when her dog died.

5. I was really (ignorant / embarrassed) when I forgot to bring a pencil to the test.

B. Match each Key Vocabulary word to the words that mean the opposite.

Example: __b__ old-fashioned

1. _____ ignorant

2. _____ depressed

3. _____ embarrassed

4. _____ obvious

5. _____ graduate

a. flunk out of school; fail

b. modern; up-to-date

c. comfortable; at ease; confident

d. hidden; subtle; invisible

e. knowledgeable; wise

f. elated; happy

C. Write sentences about yourself using Key Vocabulary words.

1. _____

2. _____

3. _____

Name _____ Date _____

● Reading Strategy
Ask Questions

Use with student book page 143.

> **Asking questions** before, while, and after you read will help you to understand the story, its characters, and how they **interact**.

Academic Vocabulary for the Reading Strategy	
Word	Explanation
interact	to communicate with someone through words or actions
tradition	a custom or belief that is passed on from one generation to another

A. Read the story below. As you read, write some facts you know in the first square of the KWL chart. Next, write two questions about what you want to know about the story or characters in the second square. Do not put anything in the third square yet.

Example:
What I Know: ___It is a story about someone named Buzzy._____

What I Know	What I Want to Know	What I Learned
1.	1.	1.
2.	2.	2.

Saturday Afternoon with Buzzy

1 Ernest learned a lot in the afternoon he spent with Buzzy. He learned patience and responsibility. He also learned the best ways to clean wood floors.

2 One day, Ernest found himself alone with Buzzy during his weekly visit to his aunt's house. She had to visit a friend in the hospital, and she had left Buzzy out of his cage. "Step up?" the small green parrot asked. For the next several hours, Ernest spent his time picking up the bird, putting the bird down, giving the bird treats, and then cleaning the treats off the floor. Ernest was exhausted. Buzzy, who was also tired, then told Ernest, "Step up!" This time it wasn't a question. Ernest took him and sat on the couch. Buzzy hopped onto Ernest's knee and nudged his hand, wanting to be scratched. As Ernest scratched his head, Buzzy puffed up, and began to fall asleep. It was the sweetest thing Ernest had ever seen. He smiled, and then he puffed up and fell asleep, too.

B. Fill in the third square of the KWL chart. Select events from the story that answer your questions. What did you learn about the characters and the story?

Name _____ Date _____

● Text Genre
Short Story

Use with student book page 144.

Short Story	
introduction	presents the characters, the setting, and the main problem in the story
rising action	the events that happen before the climax
climax	the turning point of the story
resolution	the conclusion or final result of the story

Read the story. Circle the **(introduction)**, underline the **rising action,** draw a box around the **[climax]**, and underline the **resolution** with a wavy line.

1 It was my birthday, but no one seemed to notice. My parents and my sister barely spoke to me at the breakfast table. The school day passed like any other day, and when I came home from school no one was even there to greet me.

2 Hours passed. I heard my mother come home and pots clanking in the kitchen. I heard my father come home and turn the TV on in the living room. Then my mother called me downstairs. I thought she remembered and was going to give me my gift! But when I got downstairs, her face was serious. "Your sister isn't home yet. I'm worried. I need you to go look for her." My face fell. Why should I do this on my birthday? Then I stopped and thought that maybe something happened to my sister, and I was being selfish! My mother told me to check the library first and then Aunt Martha's, which was near the library. "I tried calling Martha," Mother explained, "but she never answers the phone."

3 When I got to the library, it was just closing, so I crossed the street to Martha's house. It looked really dark, like no one was home. I was starting to worry about my sister! Where could she be? I rang the bell, discouraged. To my surprise, Martha came to the door, looking strange. "Come in!" she insisted, and I followed her into the dark living room. Suddenly, the lights flew on. "Surprise!" All of my friends and family—even my parents—were standing in the living room among balloons and decorations. They didn't forget!

Name _____ Date _____

● **Reading Comprehension** *Use with student book page 153.*

Academic Vocabulary for the Reading Comprehension Questions		
Word	**Explanation**	
evidence	Words, objects, or facts that help someone find the truth	
setting	the time and place where the events of a story take place	

A. Retell the story. Tell the story "An Hour With Abuelo" in your own words.

_____

_____

_____

_____

_____

B. Write your response. How does the setting affect the narrator's attitude at the beginning? Give evidence for your response. Have you ever been in this kind of setting? How did you feel?

_____

_____

_____

_____

_____

C. Assess the reading strategy. Look back at your KWL chart on page 143 of the student book. Did asking questions help you to understand the reading? How?

_____

_____

_____

_____

_____

Name ______________________ Date ______________

Literary Element

Plot

Use with student book page 153.

The **plot** is made up of the introduction, the rising action, the climax, and the resolution.

Read the story. Then summarize the plot in the diagram below.

1 My mother and I sat in the brightly lit emergency-room waiting room. It was 8:00. My sister had been in bike accident and was unconscious. My mother squeezed my hand, and I squeezed back, closing my eyes.

2 Nurses and doctors came and went from the room, but none of them was looking for us. I got up to get a snack from the vending machine, but I realized my stomach was too full of nervous butterflies to want to eat anything. I walked to the bathroom and back. My mother was staring out the window. She looked so tired and defeated.

3 Finally, a doctor came in. "Mrs. Casey?" he said, looking at my mother. "Could you come with me, please?" I stood up to go with her, but the doctor looked at me, then back at her, concerned. "It's OK," she said, "He can hear what you have to say." We followed the doctor into the corridor. I could feel my mother's hand trembling. "Mrs. Casey," the doctor began, his voice soft and deep, "Your daughter is badly hurt, but she is going to be OK." He smiled. My mother began crying tears of relief, and she collapsed into my arms.

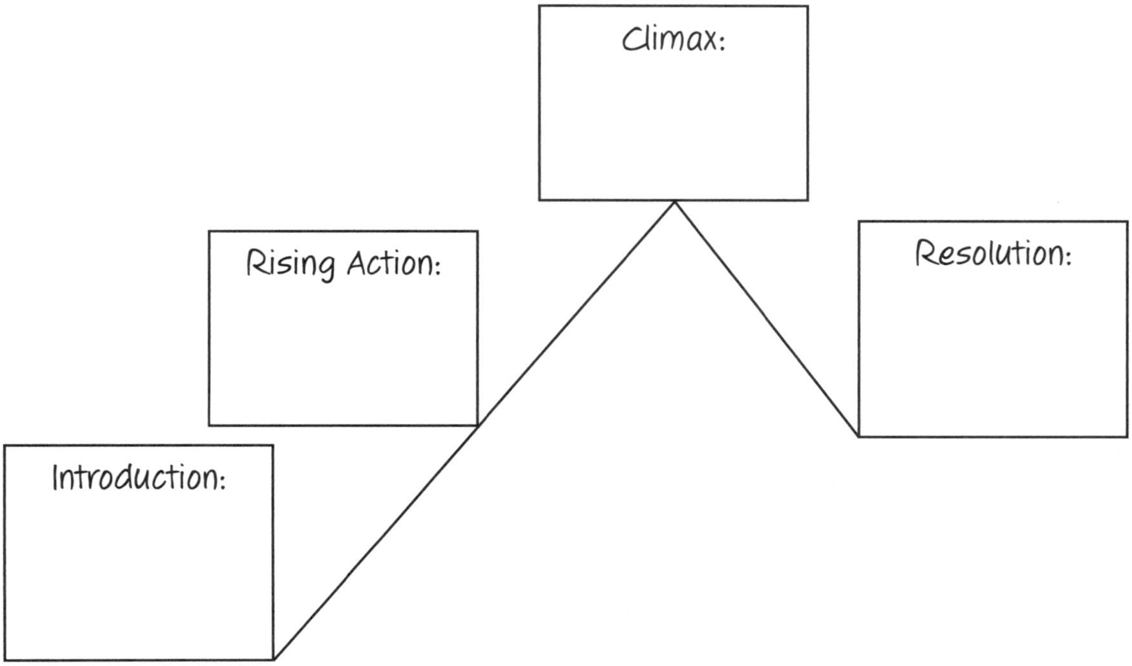

Name _____ Date _____

● **Vocabulary From the Reading**   *Use with student book page 154.*

> **Key Vocabulary**
> experiment   measure
> innate   random

A.   Complete each sentence. Use one of the Key Vocabulary words.

Example: The singer chose audience members at _____ *random* _____ to dance with her onstage.

1. The child has an _____ ability to sing. No one ever taught her!

2. My MP3 player is set to "shuffle." It plays my music in a _____ order, so I never know what song will be next!

3. I need to _____ the sofa to see how big it is. I'm not sure it will fit in our living room.

4. I'm going to do an _____: I will rub this balloon on my hair and see if it sticks to the wall.

B.   Complete the chart. Write a definition in your own words.

Example: experiment ___*a test to see if something specific happens*___

Key Vocabulary	Your Definition of the Word	
1. innate		
2. measure		
3. random		

C.   Write three sentences about your science class. Use Key Vocabulary words.

1. _____

_____

2. _____

_____

3. _____

_____

● Reading Strategy
Draw Conclusions

> You can **draw conclusions** from clues in a reading and from your own experiences.

A. Read the statement. Then answer the question.

Scientists are investigating the possibility of training dogs to detect— literally "sniff out"—cancer in humans.

What conclusion can you draw about dogs from this statement?

_____

_____

B. Read about the scientists' experiment. Then answer the questions.

The scientists exposed the rats to different amounts of sunlight each day. They recorded the rats' behavior and measured their levels of depression.

What conclusion might you draw about the scientists' objectives or motives? What conclusions might the scientists draw from their results?

_____

_____

C. Read the paragraph. Then answer the question.

The scientist studied different animals' reactions when they saw their reflections in a mirror. The cat noticed its reflection but did not seem to care. The dog barked at its reflection. The cockatiel began singing to its reflection. But the chimpanzee looked at the mirror and began using his reflection to examine the inside of his mouth. He used it to groom his head. He made funny faces and gestures at himself. He looked like he was having fun.

What conclusion can you draw about the difference between chimpanzees and the other animals?

_____

_____

Name _____   Date _____

● Text Genre

Use with student book page 155.

Informational Text: Internet Article

Web Article	
interviews	conversations in which one person asks questions and another person answers
quotes	exact statements made by a person
supporting material	evidence that proves statements are correct

Read the Internet article from FilmZone.net.

Vanessa Parker "Illuminates" Theaters

Vanessa Parker's intelligent new comedy *Illuminate Me* is popular with viewers and critics alike. The film has already made $10 million in less than a week, and ticket sales continue to rise. Critic Robert Eggers said the film "entertains and delights from beginning to end— I loved it!" João Matos of the *Somerville Sun* loved it, too, calling it a treasure. Not many critics disagreed, but one who did was Rod Lawani of the *Arlington Post,* who said, "For me, the only thing illuminating in the theater was the 'Exit' sign." (For complete reviews, click **here.**)

FilmZone spoke with the young writer and director about the film:

FilmZone: Why did you decide to make this film?

Vanessa Parker: Well, I never made a film that told *my* story. I felt that now was the right time.

F.Z.: So, the main character in this film—Carlotta— is *you*?

V.P: Yeah, more or less. I mean, it is not an exact autobiography. This is a comedy, so I took things that happened to me and made them funny.

[page **1** 2 3 4]

Decide if the following statements are **true (T)** or **false (F).** Circle the letter.

Example: Ⓣ   F   This article is on a Web site dedicated to movies.

1. T   F   This article includes quotes from movie critics.

2. T   F   This article includes an interview with the director of the film.

3. T   F   This article includes interviews with movie critics.

4. T   F   The article contains a quote from the critic João Matos.

5. T   F   The article contains supporting material for the statement that the film is popular with viewers and critics.

● Reading Comprehension

Use with student book page 161.

A. Retell the story. Summarize the main points in "It's a Math World for Animals."

_____

_____

_____

_____

_____

B. Write your response. What surprised you the most in this article? Explain.

_____

_____

_____

_____

_____

C. Assess the reading strategy. Were you able to draw conclusions using clues from the text and your own experiences? Give an example. How did this help you understand the reading?

_____

_____

_____

_____

_____

Name _____ Date _____

● Spelling
Present Participles

Use with student book page 161.

> All present participles end in **-ing**. This includes *any* verb ending in **w, x,** or **y.**
>   add**ing**, look**ing**, play**ing**, cry**ing**, show**ing**, tax**ing**
>
> If the verb ends in silent **e**, drop the **e** before adding **-ing**. If the final **e** is not silent, do not drop the **e**. If the verb ends in **-ie**, change the **ie** to **y.**
>   use⟶ us**ing**   see⟶ see**ing**, die⟶ dy**ing**
>
> For verbs ending in one vowel and one consonant:
>   If the verb has one syllable, double the final consonant.
>   run⟶ run**ning**
>   If the verb has more than one syllable, and the stress is on the last syllable, double the final consonant. Otherwise, do not.
>   for**get**⟶ forget**ting**   listen⟶ listen**ing**

A. Circle the correct present participle of the verb.

Example: Who is ((winning) / wining) the game?

1. The words are not (comeing / coming) into my head.

2. Abuelo is (writing / writting) in a notebook.

3. Are you (lieing / lying) to me?

4. My mother is always (sayying / saying), *"Así es la vida."*

5. Abuelo spent the war (moping / mopping) floors.

6. The students are (begining / beginning) to arrive.

B. Fill in the correct present participle.

Example: The kids are _____being_____ very helpful today. (be)

1. When I arrived, Abuelo was _____ in bed. (sit)

2. The dog started _____ to the ball. (swim)

3. The lady in pink was _____ bird noises. (make)

4. What is _____ in the gym? (happen)

5. Everyone is _____ poetry. (read)

6. Scientists are _____ math skills in animals. (study)

Name _____ Date _____

● Writing Conventions
Punctuation: Commas

Use with student book page 161.

Commas are used to indicate a pause in a sentence. Here are some uses of commas:

When to Use	Example
Direct address (talking directly to someone)	Arturo, look at your watch now. It's a short story, Arturo. Arturo, do you remember what day this is?
Before **please** at the end of a sentence and before or after **thank you** and **thanks**	Could you help me, please? I'll take two of those, thanks. No, thank you, sir.
After **yes**, **no**, **oh**, or **well** at the beginning of a response.	Did you see that movie? —Yes, I saw it. —Well, I am not sure if I saw it! —No, I didn't see it. —Oh, yes, it was great!

A.   Rewrite these sentences. Add commas where needed.

Example: Fatima could you come here for a minute? _Fatima, could you come_
here for a minute?

1. Arturo get that notebook from the table please. _____

_____

2. Well I am not sure Mrs. Morineaux. _____

_____

3. No thank you Melissa. _____

B.   Mark the dialogue with commas where they are needed.

Rebecca: Paul are you busy?

Paul: Yes I'm a little busy. Why do you ask Rebecca?

Rebecca: Well I need help on this math homework. Can you help me please?

Paul: Well what is the problem?

Rebecca: Oh well I don't understand how to divide fractions.

Paul: Oh I see. I can show you Rebecca. It's easy.

Rebecca: I really appreciate it thanks!

Name _____ Date _____

● Vocabulary Development
Use with student book page 163.
Idioms

> An **idiom** is a phrase, or group of words, that means something different from the literal, or real, meaning of the words in the phrase.

A. Use the clues in the sentence to guess the meaning of each underlined idiom.

Sentence	Meaning of Idiom
Example: The music at the party was so loud that I had to shout <u>at the top of my lungs</u> so my friends could hear me.	very loudly
1. My parents' new wide-screen television cost <u>an arm and a leg</u>.	
2. Don't worry about Mrs. Walsh's threats. She won't do anything to you. She's <u>all bark and no bite</u>.	
3. Stop <u>beating around the bush</u> and just get to the point—what do you want from me?	
4. I'm really tired. I'm going to <u>hit the sack</u>. Good night!	
5. Mom <u>hit the roof</u> when my sister and I broke a lamp playing soccer in the living room.	

B. Write true sentences about your own experiences using each of the idioms above or on page 163 of your student book.

Example: ___The thought of eating fast food turns my stomach.___

1. _____

2. _____

3. _____

4. _____

5. _____

6. _____

Name _____ Date _____

● **Grammar**

Conjunctions

Use with student book page 164.

Conjunction	What It Does	Example
and	connects two similar ideas	I always wanted to be a writer **and** teacher.
but	shows contrast	Abuelo wanted to be a teacher, **but** he became a farmer instead.
or	gives two different choices	Researchers can learn about people's math skills by studying those of monkeys **or** tamarins.
so (that)	gives a reason	The dog jumped into the water **so that** he could get the ball.

A. Write the correct conjunction to complete each sentence.

Example: Do you want milk ___*or*___ water with your sandwich?

1. I'm having fruit _____ yogurt mixed together for dessert.

2. I don't want to go to math class after lunch, _____ I have to.

3. I studied hard _____ I can do well on the test today.

4. After math, I have English _____ science.

5. I am not sure if I am going to walk _____ take the bus home today.

B. Write sentences about your school day using conjunctions from the above chart. Write one sentence for each conjunction.

Example: _I usually bring money so that I can buy milk in the cafeteria._

1. _____

2. _____

3. _____

4. _____

5. _____

6. _____

Name _____ Date _____

● **Grammar**   *Use with student book page 165.*

Conjunctions in Compound Sentences

Simple Sentences	Compound Sentences
He threw the ball into the water. The dog swam after it.	He threw the ball into the water, **and** the dog swam after it.
I start to push him toward the rec room. He shakes his finger at me.	I start to push him toward the rec room, **but** he shakes his finger at me.
Arturo told his mom to come back in an hour. He would take the bus home.	Arturo told his mom to come back in an hour, **or** he would take the bus home.

A. Circle the best conjunction that fits the meaning of each sentence.

Example: I tried to open the juice bottle, (and /(but)/ or) the cap was on too tightly.

1. Father told me I had to study, (and / but / or) I wouldn't pass my classes.

2. We want to go to the museum, (and / but / or) it is closed on Mondays.

3. We have plenty of time—we can go shopping, (and / but / or) then we can go to the movies.

4. We don't have a lot of time—we can go to the bookstore, (and / but / or) we can go to the shoe store.

5. We wanted to buy new running shoes, (and / but / or) they were too expensive.

B. Combine the simple sentences using the correct conjunction.

Example: You can buy that CD. You can save your money.
       You can buy that CD, or you can save your money.

1. Olivia studied very hard. She didn't pass the test. _____

_____

2. Grandfather smiled at me. I smiled back at him. _____

_____

3. I could do a research report for extra credit to get an A in the class. I could do nothing and accept my B. _____

_____

4. I go to Drama Club meetings on Tuesday afternoons. I go to Math Team practice on Wednesdays. _____

_____

Name _____ Date _____

● Grammar Expansion
Compound Conjunctions

Some conjunctions have two parts.

Conjunction	What It Does	Examples
both...and	connects two similar ideas	**Both** my brother **and** I sat at the table. He ate **both** his dinner **and** mine.
not only... but...also	connects two similar ideas	I **not only** wrote the essay, **but** I **also** wrote a letter to my grandparents.
either...or	gives two different choices	I would like **either** the turkey **or** the chicken sandwich. **Either** Janet **or** Hamid will help you.
neither...nor	gives two different choices, but is negative **Note:** The verb must be affirmative.	I want **neither** the liver **nor** the lima beans. **Neither** Samira **nor** Chris has the book.

Note: If the verb follows **or, nor,** or **but also,** it should agree with the noun or pronoun that is closer to it.

Fill in the blanks with the correct compound conjunctions.

Example: ___Either___ you will do it ___or___ your brother will do it, because someone has to do it.

1. Ioana is _____ the captain of the girls' volleyball team, _____ she's _____ a champion swimmer.

2. For tonight's special, we can order _____ marinated steak for $27.00 _____ grilled shrimp for $25.00.

3. _____ steak _____ shrimp is interesting for me; I prefer chicken.

4. _____ Arnold _____ Silvia are coming to the meeting today.

5. I _____ got a good grade on the math test today, _____ I _____ won a prize in the art contest!

6. _____ the math test _____ the social studies test was very difficult for me. I got **Bs** on both of them.

Name _____ Date _____

● Grammar Expansion
Transition Words and Expressions

Transition words link and introduce ideas.

Transition Word	What It Does	Examples
therefore so consequently	introduces a consequence	I was hungry. **Therefore,** I ate. I was hungry, **so** I made a sandwich. It rained; **consequently,** we stayed in.
furthermore in fact indeed	introduces additional related information or confirms an idea	I was hungry. **Furthermore,** I was tired. I was hungry. **In fact,** I was starving! It was raining; **indeed,** it was a bad storm.
nevertheless however	shows contrast	I was hungry; **nevertheless,** I kept working. It was raining; **however,** we went outside.

A. Circle the best transition word to complete each sentence.

Example: My bike broke; (indeed / however /(so)), I took the bus.

1. Cecilia's leg was hurt; (in fact / consequently / nevertheless), she walked home.

2. Fadi had a toothache. (However / Therefore / Indeed), he went to the dentist.

3. Louis knows a lot about birds; (nevertheless / indeed / however), he wrote a book about training and caring for parrots.

4. Denise speaks Spanish. (In fact / So / However), she is fluent.

5. Carlos plays soccer. (So / Nevertheless / Furthermore), he plays baseball and basketball.

6. Sondra was rude to her mother. (In fact / However / Consequently), she was punished.

B. Complete the following sentences.

Example: The movie is good; indeed, _it is the best movie I've seen all year_____.

1. I want a new jacket; however, _____.

2. I have homework to do; in fact, _____.

3. My friends are funny; furthermore, _____.

4. We studied a lot. Consequently, _____.

Name _____ Date _____

● Writing Assignment
Short Story

Use with student book pages 166–167.

Write a short story about something that forces a character in the story to make a choice. Make notes in the chart below to help you organize your thoughts before you write your story.

My Main Character: Describe your main character's appearance and personality.	
The Conflict: Describe the problem or situation your character faces.	
Choice: What difficult choice does your character make? Will the choice be made at the beginning of the story, or will the choice be part of the climax?	
Introduction: Sketch out the setting and background details for your introduction.	
Rising Action: What events lead up to or result from the character's choice?	
Climax: This is the turning point of the story when the decisions or actions of the main character come together. What happens?	
Resolution: How does your story end? Did your character learn a lesson? What was it?	

Name _____ Date _____

● **Writing Assignment**   *Use with student book page 167.*
Writing Support

> **Mechanics: Semicolon and Colon**
>
> A **semicolon** allows a writer to connect two independent clauses to make one sentence. A **colon** precedes a list at the end of a sentence.
>
> - A semicolon can take the place of a period between what would otherwise be two separate sentences.
> - A semicolon can be used instead of a conjunction such as *and* in a compound sentence.
> - A colon alerts the reader to an upcoming list of terms.
> - A colon can also follow introductory terms such as **the following.**

A. Fill in the blank with a semicolon or a colon.

Example: I had to stay after school _;_ I was talking too much during class.

1. Sandra went home after school ____ her field hockey practice was canceled.

2. My favorite fruits are the following ____ mangoes, guavas, and pineapples.

3. Shiraz has four brothers ____ Hatem, Mohamed, Lotfi, and Rachid.

4. Seth ate some of the banana bread ____ he didn't know that his mother had made it for the neighbors.

5. Fred has only traveled outside of the U.S. three times ____ once to Mexico, once to Canada, and once to England.

B. Combine the sentences using either a semicolon or a colon.

Example: I love peanuts. I also love raisins.
                I love peanuts; I also love raisins.

1. There are three subjects Hannah really likes. They are art, music, and English.

   _____

2. Our trip was very interesting. We traveled all over East Asia.

   _____

3. It was a very cold day. Everyone stayed inside.

   _____

4. The following are some things you should bring to the beach. You should bring a towel, sunglasses, sunscreen, and a picnic lunch. _____

   _____

Name _____   Date _____

● Writing Assignment
Revising Activity

Use with student book page 167.

Sometimes using short sentences is effective when you want to build tension or show that action is happening quickly. However, it is usually more interesting for your reader if some sentences are short and some are combined.

Short	The man in black entered the building. He climbed the stairs. He stopped at Apartment B. He looked around. He broke the lock on the door.
Short & Combined	The man in black entered the building and climbed the stairs. He stopped at Apartment B. He looked around, and then he broke the lock on the door.

Rewrite this paragraph to make it more interesting for the reader. Combine some of the sentences using conjunctions, semicolons, and colons.

Greta had a long paper to write about the founding fathers. It was due on Friday. On Monday, she should have started it. Her friend Tim invited her to his house. They watched movies. Tuesday afternoon, she had softball practice until 5:00. She didn't have time afterwards to work on the paper. On Wednesday, Greta had free time. She decided to go shopping with her friend Wendy. Thursday was her last day to work on the paper. She went to the library. She made a pile of photocopies. She also checked out three books. One was called *John Adams,* one was called *Founding Fathers: Uncommon Heroes,* and one was called *Shh! We're Writing the Constitution*. Then she went home. She watched TV for two hours. She started to write after dinner. She realized she had made a mistake. Poor Greta had to stay up all night. She could finish her paper. She finished at 7:00. She went to school. She was tired. She was sick. Her paper was not very good. She got a C-. She started her next paper the day it was assigned!

_____

_____

_____

_____

_____

_____

_____

_____

_____

_____

Name _____   Date _____

● **Writing Assignment**   *Use with student book page 167.*
Editing Activity

Read the story and find the mistakes. Mark the mistakes using the editing marks on page 455. Then rewrite the story correctly.

    They're was a very old house in my neighborhood: nobody lived their. One day, my friend Len or I decided to go inside. We took the following things with us; a flashlight, a bag, and a notebook. We found an unlocked window near the ground at the back of the house, but we squeezed inside and jumped to the floor, we were in the basement. It was very creepy there: it was dark and damp, or there were spiderwebs everywhere. We found the stairs but climbed them up to the first floor. When we opened the door, we saw a man standing their in a grey wool coat and hat. Both Len or I screamed at the top of our lungs. We turned and rushed to the front door. We not only ran out of the house; and we also ran all the way home. The next day; we learned it was just my father's friend, Hortense!

_____

_____

_____

_____

_____

_____

_____

_____

_____

_____

_____

_____

_____

_____

Name ______________________ Date ______________

Vocabulary From the Reading

Use with student book page 172.

Key Vocabulary

argument
ban
convince
guarantee
intention
possess
violate

A. Read the clues. Use the Key Vocabulary words to complete the puzzle.

Across

3. get someone to agree
4. break (a law)
6. promises
7. statement or speech meant to persuade

Down

1. forbid; make illegal
2. plan; purpose
5. own; have

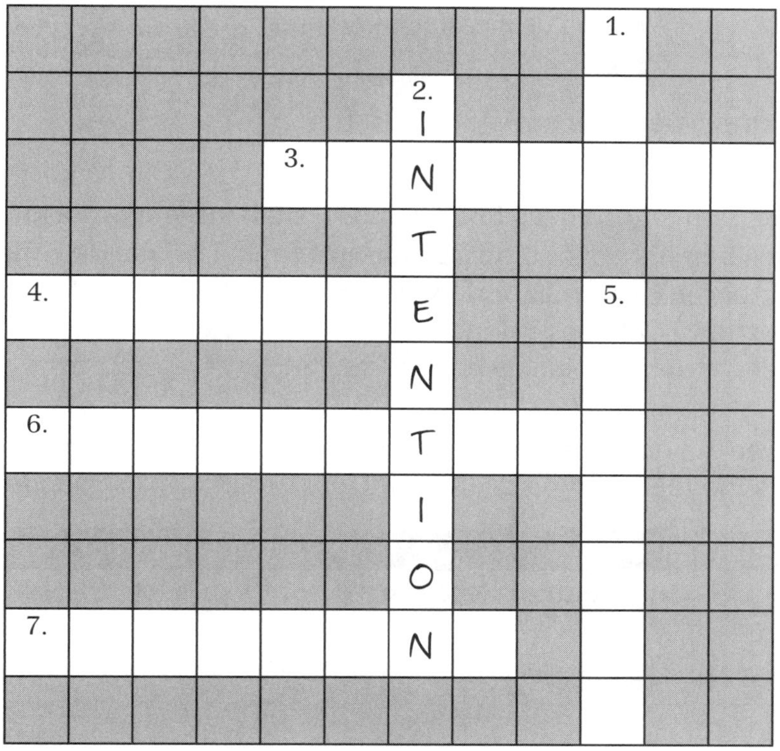

B. Answer the questions.

1. What are two things that your school has banned? ______________________

____

2. Describe a time when you convinced someone to do something. What arguments did you make? ______________________

____

Name _____   Date _____

● Reading Strategy
Analyze the Author's Purpose

Use with student book page 173.

Consider the author's thought **process** to think about his or her **purpose** in writing. Decide if the intention of the text is to inform, persuade, or entertain. Then ask yourself if your reasoning is **valid**.

Academic Vocabulary for the Reading Strategy		
Word	**Explanation**	
process	a series of actions taken to get a result	
valid	based on sensible reasoning	

Read the paragraph.

Mark Twain is one of the best-loved writers in American history. He was born Samuel Clemens in 1835 in the small town of Florida, Missouri. Twain described his birth in his autobiography: "The village contained 100 people and I increased its population by one percent. It is more than many of the best men in history could have done for a town. There is no record of a person doing as much—not even Shakespeare."

Answer the questions in the chart. Under "Author's Purpose," tell how the author wants the reader to react. Does he want to inform, persuade, or entertain?

Detail from Text	Author's Purpose
1. How does the author describe Mark Twain? one of the best-loved writers in history	_____ _____

Detail from Text	Author's Purpose
2. Where was Twain born?	_____ _____

Detail from Text	Author's Purpose
3. What does Twain say about his own birth?	_____ _____

Name _____ Date _____

● Text Genre

Use with student book page 172.

Historical Nonfiction

Historical Nonfiction	
events	what happened
dates	when the events happened
characters	real people in history who appear in the reading

A. Read the paragraph about Juneteenth. Circle the dates.

Juneteenth is an annual celebration that commemorates the freeing of the slaves in Texas at the end of the Civil War. On June 19, 1865, just two months after the assassination of Abraham Lincoln on April 14, General Gordon Granger of the Union Army arrived in Galveston, Texas, with his soldiers and read General Order Number 3, which officially freed the approximately 250,000 slaves in the state. As the news spread, the newly freed slaves rejoiced and celebrated. Lincoln's Emancipation Proclamation, issued on January 1, 1863, had declared all slaves living in the rebel Confederate states to be free; however, it did not actually change the lives of most slaves in Confederate territory until they fell under Union control. Juneteenth has been observed as a holiday by African-Americans since June of 1866, but it became an official state holiday in Texas on January 1, 1980, under Governor William P. Clements, Jr. Since then, many other states have recognized the holiday.

B. List the characters in the paragraph.

General Gordon Granger, _____

_____

C. Now summarize four important events.

_____

_____

_____

_____

_____

_____

Name _____ Date _____

● Reading Comprehension

Use with student book page 185.

Academic Vocabulary for the Reading Comprehension Questions	
Word	**Explanation**
conclusion	something you decide is true after thinking about it carefully
identify	to recognize something and be able to say what it is

A. Retell the story. Identify the main events in "The Dred Scott Decision."

_____

_____

_____

_____

_____

B. Write your response. How did the Dred Scott decision bring the United States closer to civil war? Explain your conclusion.

_____

_____

_____

_____

_____

C. Assess the reading strategy. Did identifying and analyzing the author's purpose help you understand the text better? Why or why not?

_____

_____

_____

_____

_____

Milestones C • Copyright © Heinle

● **Text Element**
Chronological Order

Use with student book page 187.

> **Chronological order** is the order in which events happen.

Reread the paragraph about Juneteenth.

    Juneteenth is an annual celebration that commemorates the freeing of the slaves in Texas at the end of the Civil War. On June 19, 1865, just two months after the assassination of Abraham Lincoln on April 14, General Gordon Granger of the Union Army arrived in Galveston, Texas, with his soldiers and read General Order Number 3, which officially freed the approximately 250,000 slaves in the state. As the news spread, the newly freed slaves rejoiced and celebrated. Lincoln's Emancipation Proclamation, issued on January 1, 1863, had declared all slaves living in the rebel Confederate states to be free; however, it did not actually change the lives of most slaves in Confederate territory until they fell under Union control. Juneteenth has been observed as a holiday by African-Americans since June of 1866, but it became an official state holiday in Texas on January 1, 1980, under Governor William P. Clements, Jr. Since then, many other states have recognized the holiday.

Complete the time line, listing the events in chronological order.

1. January 1st, 1863:	3.	5.

2.	4.

Name _____ Date _____

● Vocabulary From the Reading

Use with student book page 188.

> **Key Vocabulary**
>
> age   equally
> difference   rather

A. Complete each sentence with a Key Vocabulary word.

Example: I could watch a movie, but I would _____*rather*_____ read a book.

1. There is a big _____ between my sister and me—she is very shy and I am not.

2. When we visited the old village, I felt like we had traveled back to another

    _____.

3. I can run very fast, and my brother can run _____ fast.

B. Rewrite the sentences. Replace the underlined phrase with a Key Vocabulary word.

Example: How is Joe? I haven't seen him in <u>many years</u>!

   How is Joe? I haven't seen him in ages!

1. Would you <u>prefer to</u> go swimming or hiking?

    _____

2. I painted the old table, but it didn't make a <u>change</u>. It still looked ugly.

    _____

3. Habib plays soccer very well, and Joe plays <u>as</u> well.

    _____

C. Choose two of the Key Vocabulary words and use each of them in a sentence.

1. _____

2. _____

Name _____ Date _____

● Reading Strategy
Recognize Symbols

Use with student book page 189.

> A **symbol** is an object that can take on the meaning of a different idea.

Read the poem.

> A fire raged and burned my heart,
> And flames flew from my tongue,
> I shot at you a flaming dart
> And cared not if it stung.
>
> I couldn't see through all the smoke,
> That hung before my eyes;
> I couldn't hear when people spoke,
> But then came a surprise:
>
> Your tears fell from the cloudy skies,
> I felt my fire dying;
> The smoke cleared from my ears and eyes,
> And I could see you crying.
>
> And after fire and rain had gone,
> The sky was blue and fair,
> I found a flower, white as dawn,
> And put it in your hair.

Choose the best answer to complete each statement.

Example: __b__ The fire here is a symbol of _____.
a. warmth   b. anger   c. love

1. _____ The flames that fly from the narrator's tongue are _____.
a. mean words   b. poems   c. actual flames

2. _____ The narrator can't see because _____.
a. there is too much smoke   b. the skies are cloudy   c. he is too angry

3. _____ The girl's tears are compared to _____.
a. dawn   b. rain   c. cloudy skies

4. _____ The fair blue sky is a symbol of _____.
a. good weather   b. sadness   c. calm emotions

5. _____ The flower is a symbol of _____.
a. crying   b. a peace offering   c. a nice decoration

Name _____ Date _____

● **Text Genre**   *Use with student book page 189.*
Poetry

Poetry		
element	rhyming poetry	free verse poetry
rhyming words at the ends of lines	yes	not usually
lines of about the same number of syllables	yes	no
stanzas with the same number of lines	usually	not always

Analyze this poem's features and answer the question below.

A golden leaf fell off a tree
And landed right in front of me.
I took it home and laid it down;
In three days it was dry and brown.

I plucked a rose of petals soft
And gave it to you, held aloft.
I wonder, has that rose since died,
Its brittle petals brown and dried?

1. What kind of poem is it? How do you know? Give examples of each feature.

_____

_____

_____

Heavily we go up the rocky slope,
Though we are careful,
We are weary and look only at our feet.

Why can we not look up?
Is it fog or fair skies over the mountain's peak?

2. What kind of poem is it? How do you know? Give examples of each feature.

_____

_____

_____

Name _____ Date _____

● Reading Comprehension

Use with student book page 193.

A. Retell the story. Describe the poems by Robert Frost and Diana Chang.

"The Road Not Taken":

_____

_____

_____

"Saying Yes":

_____

_____

_____

B. Write your response. Which poem did you relate to more? Why?

_____

_____

_____

_____

_____

C. Assess the reading strategy. How does recognizing symbols help you to understand a poem? Give an example from one of the two poems in this chapter.

_____

_____

_____

_____

_____

Name _____ Date _____

● Spelling
Silent letters: k, gh, h, l, b

Use with student book page 193.

In English, there are many letters or letter combinations that are silent in some words and not silent in other words. Here are some examples:

Letter(s)	Silent	Not Silent
gh	eight, right, sigh, night, light, caught, thought, though, through	ghost, spaghetti (hard *g* sound) cough, laugh (*f* sound)
h	white, whether, whispery, hours	who, how, half, have, house
k	knowing, knee, knife, knead, knight, knot, knit	kick, kitten, black, ask, took
l	could, should, would, walk, talk, chalk, half, calf	library, lemon, clap, wall, milk cold, shoulder
b	doubt, plumber, thumb, numb, dumb, lamb, bomb, climb	bird, stumble, lab, number, chamber, member

A. Silent or not silent? Check if the **bolded** letter or letter combination is silent.

1. ✓ whispered
2. ____ knowledge
3. ____ laughter
4. ____ ghostly
5. ____ thoughtful
6. ____ walking
7. ____ help
8. ____ milky
9. ____ doubtful
10. ____ mumble
11. ____ crib
12. ____ although

B. Fill in the missing silent letters.

It was a dark Friday ni_gh_t, and there was a ha____f moon shining dimly like a w____ite thum____nail in the sky. I was wa____king home from my aunt's house, and I had to cut throu____ the creepy old cemetery. I didn't ____now the way very well, and there was not very much li____t, so I couldn't see. My foot got cau____t in some tree roots, and I fell and hurt my ____nee. While I was on the ground, I thou____t I heard voices w____ispering and ta____king behind me. I was so scared that I felt num____, but I got up and ran all the way home on my sore leg.

Name _____ Date _____

● Writing Conventions
Punctuation: Colons

Use with student book page 193.

In Chapter 1, you learned that colons can be used to introduce a list. Here are some more uses for colons.

To introduce an explanation or revelation (after an independent clause)	Finally, Taney answered one last question: Was Dred Scott free because he had lived in the free state of Illinois?
	There was just one thing I needed to make my Saturday afternoon complete: a book!
To introduce a direct quotation	The *Chicago Tribune* was at a loss for words: "We scarcely know how to express our disgust."

Note: When the text after a colon is an independent clause, the first letter should be capitalized.

A. Add colons where they are needed. Use editing marks to show where to insert the colons.

Example: There was one thing missing from my sandwich: the cheese.

1. Mr. Baxter had an unexpected reply when we asked him what he thought of the show "I've never seen anything so silly in my entire life!"

2. Sue read the last line of the poem "And that has made all the difference."

3. I wanted to tell Anna my secret, but I knew what would happen she would tell her sister, and by the next day the whole school would know.

4. I saw that sitting next to me was the one person I feared Scott McCann.

B. Expand the following sentences by adding a colon and information from the student book readings.

Example: The *Constitutionalist* thought that the South had won a victory. (page 183, paragraph 24)

   The Constitutionalist thought that the South had won a victory: "Southern opinion upon the subject of slavery . . . is now the law of the land."

1. In the last line of her poem, Diana Chang summarizes how she wants to answer questions about her nationality. (page 192) _____

_____

2. The *Louisville Democrat* agreed with the Dred Scott decision. (page 183, paragraph 24) _____

_____

Name _____ Date _____

● Vocabulary Development
Use with student book page 195.

Denotative and Connotative Meanings

> The **denotative meaning** of a word is its actual meaning. The **connotative meaning** of a word is the images or feelings we attach to the word.

A. Put the following meanings in the correct place in the chart below.

the end of something	ocean	peace
a white bird	sadness or ignorance	shadow; absence of light
rock	brightness	cold; unfeeling; hard
hope; happiness; wisdom	something vast, immense	when the sun goes down

Word	Denotative Meaning	Connotative Meaning
1. sunset	when the sun goes down	_____
2. light	_____	_____
3. darkness	_____	_____
4. sea	_____	_____
5. dove	_____	_____
6. stone	_____	_____

B. Check each sentence that uses the **connotative** meaning of the word in **bold**.

Example: __✔__ The actress was in the **sunset** of her career.

1. _____ My friend has a pet **dove.**

2. _____ Principal Graves had a heart of **stone.**

3. _____ Wendy is facing a **sea** of troubles.

4. _____ We used a candle to make our way through the **darkness** of the forest.

5. _____ My mother is the **light** of my life.

Name _____ Date _____

● Grammar

Use with student book page 196.

Complex Sentences

A **complex sentence** is one or more dependent clauses joined by a subordinating conjunction.

Subordinating Conjunction	What It Shows	Example
after, before, when	time	**After** he visited his grandfather, Arturo understood him better. Arturo didn't know much about his grandfather **before** he visited him at the nursing home. I'm about to ask him why he didn't keep fighting to make his dream come true **when** an old lady appears at the door.
because	reason	**Because** the experiment with primates and babies was successful, Uller wanted to try the same experiment with salamanders.
although	contrast	I felt like a rich man **although** the pay was very small.
if	condition	**If** you give babies a choice of two or three items, they'll choose three.

A. Circle the correct subordinating conjunction to complete each sentence.

Example: I fell asleep (although / before /(because)) I was exhausted.

1. (Before / Because / Although) he went to bed, Boris brushed his teeth.

2. You will get hungry (if / before / although) you don't eat breakfast.

3. Hermann ate his sandwich (if / although / because) he wasn't hungry.

4. (When / If / Although) she got home, Susana began studying.

5. (After / Although / If) we finished the test, the teacher let us leave the classroom.

B. Write complete sentences. Use the following phrases to start them.

1. If I don't exercise, _____

2. Although I am very young, _____

3. When I get home from school, _____

4. Because I work hard, _____

Name _____ Date _____

● **Grammar**   *Use with student book page 197.*
Compound-Complex Sentences

A **compound-complex sentence** has one or more dependent clauses and two or more independent clauses. Notice the position of the clauses and the punctuation in these examples.

Dependent Clause	Independent Clause (1)	Independent Clause (2)
Because the first experiment didn't work,	the scientists wanted to try it again;	but once again it failed.

Independent Clause (1)	Dependent Clause	Independent Clause (2)
The scientists wanted to try the experiment again	because it didn't work the first time;	but once again it failed.

Add conjunctions to make the sentences logical. Choose from the following conjunctions: **although, because, if, when, before, after, but, and.**

Example: _____*Although*_____ it was late _____*and*_____ we were

tired, we stayed up playing games; _____*but*_____ the next day at school, we regretted it!

1. _____ you study hard, you will learn more;

   _____ you will do well on the test!

2. _____ we wanted to eat pizza, we ate the stew that mother

   served us; _____ we weren't happy about it.

3. _____ I arrived at the party, there were many kids there;

   _____ I didn't see Andrea.

4. _____ it was raining and there was lightning nearby, we all

   stayed inside the house; _____ we had a lot of fun playing
   board games and reading stories.

5. _____ I wanted to be polite, I ate the food Ms. Hill served me;

   _____ I didn't like it.

6. The teacher was angry at me _____ I didn't complete the

   homework assignment; _____, she told me I could stay after
   class to finish it.

Name _____ Date _____

● Grammar Expansion

Use with student book page 197.

Show Contrast and Cause: despite, in spite of, because of

Another way of combining ideas and varying sentence types is to use these expressions:

Expression	What It Shows	Example	Compare to Subordinating Conjunction
because of + noun	cause or reason	**Because of** the cold weather, we wore our coats.	Because it was cold, we wore our coats.
despite, in spite of + noun or + **the fact that** . . .	contrast	**Despite** the cold weather, we ate our lunch outside.	Although it was cold, we ate our lunch outside.
		Mother went to work **in spite of** her illness.	Mother went to work although she was ill.
		I said "yes" **despite** the fact that I didn't agree.	I said "yes" although I didn't agree.

A. Fill in the blank with **although, because, because of, in spite of,** or **despite.**

Example: I called my friend's house _____ *although* _____ it was after midnight.

1. My friend answered the phone _____ the late hour.

2. The baseball game was canceled _____ the rain.

3. We went for a walk outside _____ the rain.

4. _____ it was raining, we took our umbrellas with us.

5. _____ the fact that I am much younger than my sister, we are very close.

B. Rewrite the sentences using **despite, in spite of,** or **because of** followed by a noun.

Example: Although it was hot, we still went jogging.

In spite of the heat, we still went jogging.

1. I couldn't play soccer because I had a sore leg.

_____

2. Suzy stayed at school although her tooth was broken.

_____

3. Although Derek has a negative attitude, he has a lot of friends.

_____

Name _____ Date _____

● Grammar Expansion

Link Ideas: in addition to, instead of, rather than, in order to

Expression	What it Shows	Example
in addition to + noun or + verb ending in **-ing**	similar idea, something extra	**In addition to** chicken, we also have fish. We often swim **in addition to** running, dancing, and lifting weights.
instead of, rather than + noun or + verb ending in **-ing**	alternative or replacement	I'll order the soup **instead of** the salad. **Rather than** taking the bus and spending $2.00, I will walk home.
in order to + verb	purpose, intention	**In order to** stay healthy, you should eat more vegetables and whole grains.

A. Fill in the blanks with the correct expressions from the chart above.

Example: Stan has to work two jobs _____in order to_____ pay his bills.

1. I think I will go to bed early _____ staying up late again.

2. At the amusement park there is so much to do: we can ride the roller coaster

   _____ the bumper cars and the Ferris wheel!

3. _____ eating cereal in the morning, Frances also drinks fresh

   orange juice.

4. _____ writing your essay in your notebook and then typing

   it, why don't you simply write it on my computer?

5. _____ get to school on time, we have to wake up at 6:00 A.M.

B. Rewrite the following sentences using the expression in parentheses.

Example: Barthe likes reading. He doesn't like to watch TV.

   Barthe likes reading rather than watching TV.

1. I would like to drink milk. I don't want juice. (rather than)

   _____

2. I want to buy a new notebook. I need to ask my mother for money. (in order to)

   _____

Name _____ Date _____

● Writing Assignment
Expository Essay

Use with student book page 198.

Fill in this chart to help you prewrite your essay. Describe the characteristics of the two poetry styles you studied in this chapter. To illustrate each characteristic, give examples from the two poems in your student book or from other poems you find. You can also make up your own examples.

I. Type of Poetry: Lyric Poetry	
A. Characteristic: rhyming words	Examples:
B. Characteristic:	Examples:
C. Characteristic:	Examples:

II. Type of Poetry:	
A. Characteristic:	Examples:
B. Characteristic:	Examples:
C. Characteristic:	Examples:

Name _____ Date _____

● Writing Assignment

Use with student book page 199.

Writing Support

> **Grammar: Varying Sentences for Style**
>
> When you write, it is important to use different types of sentences. This can help you connect your ideas together better, and it can also help you hold the interest of the reader.
>
> **Simple** sentences can help you state your main idea clearly or make a strong point.
> **Compound** sentences can help you give information.
> **Complex** sentences can help you make logical connections in your writing through the use of conjunctions such as *because, although, when,* and *after.*
> **Compound-complex** sentences work like complex sentences, but by adding extra independent clauses, you can put additional information into your sentence.

Read the paragraph. Rewrite it using a variety of sentence styles. Try to have at least one use of each style from the box above.

   We read Jennifer Trujillo's poem "The Mosaic of English" in Unit 2. We read two poems in Unit 3. We learned about different styles of poetry. We can analyze the style of Trujillo's poem based on this information. Trujillo's poem is a kind of lyric poem. It has rhyming words at the end of its lines. It has lines with more or less the same number of syllables. Trujillo's poem is less serious in tone than Robert Frost's poem. She does not use a lot of symbols. She uses humor. Trujillo's poem is long and is not free verse. Her poem has one thing in common with Diana Chang's poem. She writes from the perspective of a girl caught between two cultures.

_____

_____

_____

_____

_____

_____

_____

_____

_____

Name _____ Date _____

● Writing Assignment
Revising Activity

Use with student book page 199.

Read each Revision Tip. Then rewrite the sentences to make them better.

Revision Tip # 1: Be accurate and avoid opinions. You are writing an expository essay, which means you are giving an informative description and analysis. A persuasive essay would be a more appropriate place for expressing your opinions.

First Try	A Better Way to Say It
Example: Lyric poems are more fun than free verse poems.	Lyric poems are more structured than free verse poems.
1. I don't understand many of the symbols in poetry.	
2. I like free verse poems because the poets can just write whatever they want.	
3. Diana Chang's poem is much easier to understand than Robert Frost's poem.	

Revision Tip # 2: Use specific examples to clarify or support your points.

First Try	A Better Way to Say It
1. A rhyme is a pair of words that sound similar.	
2. The roads in Frost's poem are a symbol.	
3. Free verse poems have no structure.	

Name _____ Date _____

● Writing Assignment
Editing Activity

Use with student book page 199.

Read the paragraph. Correct the errors in spelling, punctuation, and word usage using the editing marks on page 455. Then rewrite the paragraph correctly.

     Although I worked for hours last nite on my essay about poetry I didn't finish it. Because I had a hard time understanding the poems. One of the poems was "My Dream: A Vision of Peace" by Toddmichael St. Pierre. And the other was a poem by my teacher, called "Doves." Despite I was nervous I was surprised by the reaction of my teacher this morning she was not angry. Instead of give me a bad grade she offered to tak with me about the poems after class. I finally understood the poem she wrote if she explained the first two lines to me and the other poem was also not as difficult as I thout. After taking with my teacher I now what both poems mean and I can write my essay. There is only one thing to worry about now will I write a good essay?

_____

_____

_____

_____

_____

_____

_____

_____

_____

_____

_____

_____

_____

_____

_____

_____

Name _____ Date _____

● Vocabulary From the Reading

Use with student book page 216.

> **Key Vocabulary**
>
> disgrace   promotion
> etiquette   spectacle
> progress   stalk

A. Read the sentence. Then write the letter for the correct meaning of the Key Vocabulary word.

My little brother's lack of <u>etiquette</u> <u>disgraced</u> us at the party. He put two <u>stalks</u> of asparagus in his ears. He thought it was funny, but he made a <u>spectacle</u> of us all.

Example: __*c*__ The word **stalks** refers to

     a. a supply   b. a type of walk   c. long stem of a plant

1. _____ In this paragraph, **etiquette** means

     a. a ticket   b. manners or politeness   c. knowledge

2. _____ In this paragraph, **disgraced** means

     a. embarrassed   b. amused, entertained   c. honored

3. _____ If the boy made a **spectacle** of his family, it means

     a. they were wearing glasses   b. everyone was looking at them
     c. he gave them a gift

B. Fill in the missing Key Vocabulary words.

My aunt got a job in a restaurant last year. She has made a lot of

(1) _____ there. They gave her a (2) _____:

She is now the head chef. She has added many (3) _____

to the menu.

C. Write three sentences about eating customs in your country. Use Key Vocabulary words in your sentences.

1. _____

2. _____

3. _____

Name _____ Date _____

● Reading Strategy
Make Inferences

Use with student book page 217.

> When you **make inferences,** you connect details from the story with your experiences and knowledge so that you can **assume** what the author's hidden message is.

Academic Vocabulary for the Reading Strategy	
Word	**Explanation**
infer	to make a guess about something that is unknown using some information that is known
assume	to believe something is true without knowing for sure

As you read the following passage, think about your own experiences and knowledge. Put the text details and your knowledge together. What can you assume about the main characters and the story events?

When we visited our family in Sweden, I was ten years old. On our first night, we had dinner at my cousin Hans's house. He served us roasted chicken with potatoes in cream sauce. My parents were embarrassed when I picked up the chicken leg from my plate and began eating it with my hands, but Hans gave me a friendly smile and told me not to worry. He handed me a napkin.

Now complete the charts.

Details from the story		Your experience and knowledge		Inference
Narrator eats chicken with hands				
	+		=	

Name _____ Date _____

● **Text Genre**

Use with student book page 218.

Autobiographical Short Story

Autobiographical Short Story	
characters	people in a story
setting	when and where the events take place
figurative language	language that goes beyond the literal meaning of words in order to help the reader see an idea or subject in a new way

A. In the following paragraphs, check off sentences that contain figurative language.

1.

> **(Example)** ✔ Mr. Jenkins, our neighbor, is a robot. (1) ____ He doesn't smile or show very much emotion. (2) ____ He is very organized and always arrives exactly on time for everything. (3) ____ He zips mechanically to and from work every day, but on the weekends his systems recharges.

2.

> (1) ____ Meg is really funny. (2) ____ She is a clown! (3) ____ She is always telling jokes. (4) ____ Her jokes kill me!

B. Read the following sentences with figurative language in bold. Match the figurative language on the left with the literal language on the right.

Example: __f__ I **was crushed** when I heard that I failed the test.

1. ____ My **blood was boiling** as I dialed his phone number.	a. I was in a hurry.
2. ____ My **heart melted** when the baby puppy licked my hand and looked up at me.	b. I felt embarrassed.
3. ____ I **flew** down the street after the bus.	c. I was very happy.
4. ____ I was **walking on air** all day after I won the contest.	d. I was emotionally affected.
5. ____ My **cheeks were burning** when I gave my report in front of the class.	e. I felt angry.
	f. I felt very sad.

Name _____ Date _____

● **Reading Comprehension**   *Use with student book page 230.*

Academic Vocabulary for Reading Comprehension Questions		
Word	**Explanation**	
indicate	to show or suggest that something else is true	
challenge	a difficult task	

A. **Retell the story.** Include specific examples of the challenges that both the Lin and the Gleason families face. What do their responses to the challenges indicate about the characters?

_____

_____

_____

_____

_____

B. **Write your response.** Have you ever faced a challenge similar to the Lins' challenge? Give specific details.

_____

_____

_____

_____

C. **Assess the reading strategy.** As you read "The All-American Slurp," you were asked to make inferences about the story based on details in the story and your own experiences. How did this help you understand the story?

_____

_____

_____

_____

Name _____ Date _____

● Literary Element

Use with student book page 231.

Figurative Language

Figurative language is language that helps the reader see things in new, interesting ways. Figurative language is imaginative. It is not meant to be read as literal. Literal means keeping the exact meaning of a word or phrase.

These are some different types of figurative language.

> **simile:** a comparison of two different things that uses the words **like** or **as**.
>
> **metaphor:** a direct comparison of two different things.
>
> **hyperbole:** a figure of speech which is an exaggeration
>
> **onomatopoeia:** The use of a word whose sound imitates its meaning.

Read the story.

(1) Mother sat sipping a cup of coffee while Father read a magazine. (2) We had just arrived back to the U.S. from the Caribbean, where we had spent our vacation. (3) Now we sat in a busy airport restaurant while we waited for our connecting flight to Washington. (4) There were about a million people eating there, and only one waitress, it seemed. (5) So, we had to wait ages for our food. (6) Finally, the nervous waitress ran to our table and threw our plates and silverware down—**slam! bang! clink!**—then she rushed away to another table.

(7) I looked down at my plate with a sigh. (8) My burger looked like a flat, grey stone resting on a soggy, white pillow. (9) My fries were strings of oily, yellow leather. (10) Reluctantly, I ate them because I was as hungry as an ox!

Now rewrite one sentence from the story that uses each type of figurative language below.

1. Simile: _____

   _____

2. Metaphor: _____

   _____

3. Hyperbole: _____

   _____

4. Onomatopoeia: _____

   _____

Name _____ Date _____

● Vocabulary From the Reading

Use with student book page 232.

> **Key Vocabulary**
> ceremony   enlightening
> complexity   restriction
> determination   transform
> enhance

A. Write the Key Vocabulary word for each definition.

Example: _____*enhance*_____ to add; to improve

Word	Definition
1. _____	to change; to evolve
2. _____	difficulty; intricacy; complicatedness
3. _____	resolve; strong decision to do something
4. _____	limitation; rule; regulation
5. _____	traditional event; ritual
6. _____	informative; educational; eye-opening

B. Complete each sentence. Use one of the Key Vocabulary words.

Example: Our school has a _____*restriction*_____ against cell phones in class.

1. Our science class today was _____: I learned a lot about animals!

2. My sister's wedding _____ was very short, but beautiful!

3. You can _____ your oral report by using good visual aids.

4. We are going to _____ our English classroom into a theater when we perform the play on Friday.

5. The _____ of the story made it very difficult to understand.

● **Reading Strategy**   *Use with student book page 233.*
Visualize

> When you **visualize,** you form images in your mind of what you are reading. You
> also imagine how things sound, smell, taste, and feel. This helps you understand and
> enjoy what you are reading.

Read the paragraph.

In the kitchen, you can hear metal whisks and bowls clang together and the
voices of the kids laughing as they roll out the soft, yellow dough to make cookies
for the class party. Some kids are cutting the dough into the shape of stars, half-
moons, and circles. The delicious smell of cookies fills the warm air as one batch
bakes. Other kids decorate a batch of crisp, golden brown cookies that have come
out of the oven. They paint complex designs on them with frosting in white, blue,
green, yellow, and pink. One kid secretly tastes a buttery cookie when no one is
looking. The group leader sees him and shouts at him, but she is not really angry.

A. Draw a picture of what you visualized when you read the paragraph.

B. In the chart, write some of the words that helped you visualize the paragraph.

Sight	Sound	Smell	Taste	Feel
kids making cookies				

Name _____ Date _____

● **Text Genre**

Use with student book page 233.

Expository Text

Expository Text		
formal style	serious tone	
facts	information that can be proven	

Read the paragraphs below. Decide whether each one is an expository text or not. Explain your reasoning.

Example: There is one painting at the museum that I think is very beautiful. It's a really tall oil painting of a woman in pink dancing with a bearded man. It looks like they're having fun. You should go and see it!

This text is not expository because it contains and informal language.

1. Sculpture is an art form that has existed for thousands of years. Sculptures can be made from many materials using different techniques.

   _____

   _____

   _____

2. Math is the hardest subject at school. It's interesting, and it's fun to solve problems, but sometimes the problems are too complex. There is only one correct answer to a math problem, so you always need to be very precise and specific. If you have one part wrong, you have the whole answer wrong.

   _____

   _____

   _____

3. Algebra is a kind of mathematics that involves balancing equations. The word **algebra** comes from an Arabic word, **al-jabr,** which appeared in ninth century Islamic texts.

   _____

   _____

   _____

● Reading Comprehension

Use with student book page 239.

A. **Retell the story.** Summarize the main ideas presented by the author in "Mathematics and Origami."

_____

_____

_____

_____

_____

B. **Write your response.** What origami figure would you like to make? How would knowing math help you make it?

_____

_____

_____

_____

_____

C. **Assess the reading strategy.** As you read "Mathematics and Origami," you were asked to visualize what the author described. How did visualizing the text help you understand it?

_____

_____

_____

_____

_____

Name _____ Date _____

● Spelling

Use with student book page 239.

Frequently Confused Words

Word	Sometimes Confused With
dessert (n.) a sweet food at the end of a meal	**desert** (v.) to abandon; (n.) an arid, sandy region
except (prep.) with the exclusion or exception of; not including	**accept** (v.) to receive or admit
stalk (n.) the stem of a plant	**stock** (n.) a supply; (v.) to keep a supply
heard (v.) past tense of *hear*	**herd** (n.) a group of animals, such as cows
tail (n.) the back end (of an animal, vehicle, tuxedo jacket)	**tale** (n.) a story
feet (n.) plural of *foot*	**feat** (n.) an accomplishment
angle (n.) a corner; figure formed by two lines coming together at a point	**angel** (n.) a spiritual being; a person who is very good
plane (n.) a flat surface; an airplane	**plain** (adj.) ordinary

A.   Choose the correctly spelled word to complete each statement.

Example: Finishing that 500-page book in two days was an amazing (feet /(feat)).

1.   The waiter who served dinner wore a (plain / plane) jacket, but the one who served (dessert / desert) wore a fancy jacket with (tales / tails).

2.   Everyone took one (stalk / stock) of celery (except / accept) my brother.

3.   Have you ever (herd / heard) the (tail / tale) "The All-American Slurp?"

4.   A square has four right (angels / angles).

5.   I jumped to my (feat / feet) and went to the ladies' room.

6.   The baby was sleeping like a little (angel / angle).

7.   The store would not (except / accept) my mother's credit card.

B.   Choose two words from each column in the chart and use them in true sentences about yourself or your experiences.

1.   _____

2.   _____

3.   _____

4.   _____

● Writing Conventions
Spelling: The Suffix -y

Use with student book page 239.

The suffix **-y** is often added to a noun to form an adjective. The **-y** means "full of, having the quality of, or characterized by." Note: Sometimes the spelling of the noun changes slightly when a suffix is added.

Noun	Meaning	-y Adjective	Meaning
murk	darkness; gloom	murky	dark; unclear; characterized by murk
zing	sharp flavor; excitement	zingy	sharp; having zing
risk	danger	risky	dangerous; characterized by risk
shake	move about	shaky	unsteady; characterized by shaking

A. Fill in the missing adjective ending in **-y.**

Example: A sky full of clouds is _____cloudy_____.

1. A beach with a lot of rocks is _____.

2. If a girl has curls, she has _____ hair.

3. A day with a lot of wind is a _____ day.

4. If there is too much salt in the food, it's _____.

5. Someone who feels a lot of anger is an _____ person.

B. Write a sentence with the **-y** adjective form of each noun given.

Example: (cream) ___The pudding was creamy and delicious.___

1. (hunger) _____

2. (spice) _____

3. (sun) _____

4. (fog) _____

5. (sugar) _____

Name _____ Date _____

● Vocabulary Development

Use with student book page 241.

Words and Phrases from Mythology

> Some words and phrases come from Greek, Latin, and Anglo-Saxon mythology.

A. Read the English words and their definitions in the chart. Then match the mythological characters with the correct description below the chart.

English Word	Definition	Mythological Character	Letter of Description
narcissist	an egotistical person; someone who is obsessed with himself or herself	Narcissus	Example: __f__
odyssey	a great journey or adventure	Odysseus	1. _____
atlas	a book containing maps of the world	Atlas	2. _____
January	the first month of the year	Janus	3. _____
go berserk	to go crazy; to lose control	Berserker	4. _____
siren	a loud, wailing alarm	Siren	5. _____

a. In Greek mythology, a man who travels and has fantastical adventures.

b. In Norse mythology, a wild warrior.

c. Roman god of beginnings and endings.

d. In Greek mythology, a woman of the sea who sings. When sailors hear her, they follow the sound to their deaths.

e. In Greek mythology, a giant who holds up the sky on his shoulders.

f. ~~In Greek mythology, a young man who falls in love with his reflection in a pond.~~

B. Describe the following situations. Use words from the chart above.

1. That girl only thinks about how she looks.

   She is a _____.

2. This is a book of maps of all the countries in the world.

   It is an _____.

3. Your friends went on a long and dangerous trip into the Amazon rain forest.

   They went on an _____.

4. Your friend was very upset because she couldn't find her cell phone.

   She went _____.

Name _____ Date _____

● Grammar

Use with student book page 242.

Prepositional Phrases

When you want to tell when, where, or how something happens, you can use a **prepositional phrase.** A prepositional phrase is made up of a **preposition** and an **object.** Some prepositions are: **about, at, down, for, from, in, on, out of, to,** and **with.**

Prepositional Phrases		
	preposition	object
The soup arrived	in	a plate.
I turned to look	at	Mrs. Gleason.
We had emigrated	from	China.

A. Underline the prepositional phrase(s) and circle the preposition(s) in each sentence.

Example: They went (from) one store (to) another store.

1. I bought a milkshake for Meg.

2. She took the pen in her hand.

3. At six o'clock, dinner is always on the table.

4. Origami is the art of paper-folding from Japan.

5. Buddhist monks brought origami from China to Japan.

6. In a reading by Theoni Pappas, we learned about origami.

B. Complete the sentences with prepositional phrases.

Example: His coat was _in a closet at his house._

1. I live _____.

2. I study _____.

3. My parents are _____.

4. We eat dinner _____.

5. I read a book _____.

6. Sometimes I go _____.

Name _____ Date _____

● Grammar

Use with student book page 243.

Appositives

When you want to add more information about a noun or pronoun, you can use an **appositive**. An **appositive** is a noun or noun phrase that is placed next to another noun to help describe or explain it. For example,

Anna's sister, **that woman with the red hair,** is having a party Saturday.

Sentences with Appositives		
noun	**appositive**	
Quentin,	**my brother,**	flew in an airplane for the first time yesterday.
Stan,	**the school's bus driver,**	is moving to Nebraska.
My teacher,	**Ms. Moran,**	is going to have a talk with my mother.

A.   Combine the sentences. Use an appositive.

Example: Julia once climbed that tree. Julia is my sister.
Julia, my sister, once climbed that tree.

1. Carlos is coming to the baseball game. Carlos is the new student.

    _____

2. Wendy has a traditional dress from Mexico. Wendy is my sister.

    _____

3. My lunch today is nutritional. My lunch is a tuna sandwich.

    _____

4. Our dog is very friendly. Our dog is a black Labrador retriever.

    _____

B.   Write four sentences about your friends and family using appositives.

1. _____

2. _____

3. _____

4. _____

Name _____ Date _____

● Grammar Expansion

Phrasal Verbs

Some verbs take a special meaning when followed by another word called an adverbial particle. The meaning of the verb changes depending on the adverbial particle.

Verb	Phrasal Verb	Phrasal Verb
get	**get up:** to rise *We got up and walked to the buffet table.*	**get on** (a vehicle): to embark; to enter *Meg and I got on the school bus together.*
give	**give up:** to quit; to admit defeat *He tried to understand the French menu, but he finally gave up.*	**give off** (something): to emit; to radiate (such as light, heat, an odor, a signal) *The food gave off a wonderful aroma.*
look	**look up*** (something): to search for something in a dictionary or other source *Father looked up the items on the menu that were in French.*	**look on:** to observe *Everyone looked on as we made a spectacle of ourselves at the dinner party.*
pick	**pick up*** (something or someone): to retrieve; to go and get; to lift *Mr. Gleason picked up the pea with his fingers.*	**pick out*** (something): to select *I had to pick out a nice outfit to wear to the fancy restaurant.*

*These phrasal verbs are separable by nouns and pronouns: **look the word up, pick them up, pick one out**

A. Circle the correct verb or phrasal verb to complete each statement.

Example: I fell down the stairs as everyone (looked /(looked on)).

1. We each (picked / picked up) a different kind of cheese from the tray.

2. I had to (look / look up) information about origami on the Internet.

3. Sheila (gets on / gets up) every morning at 6:00.

4. We (got on / got up) the bikes and rode away quickly.

5. After five minutes of trying to open the jar, mother (gave off / gave up).

6. The rotten fish (gave / gave off) a horrible smell.

7. You should (look up / look on) that word in the dictionary.

8. I (gave up / gave off) eating sugar because it is unhealthy.

Name _____ Date _____

● Grammar Expansion

Nonrestrictive Clauses with which, who, whom, and whose

When you want to add more information about a noun, you can use an appositive or a **nonrestrictive clause**—a phrase that is placed next to a noun to help describe or explain it. A nonrestrictive clause gives more information than an appositive:

Word	What It Describes	Example
which	a thing	The book is interesting. I read it last year. The book, **which** I read last year, is interesting.
who	a person (subject)	Erik has fun parties. He is from Norway. Erik, **who** is from Norway, has fun parties.
whom	a person (object)	Cindy is really nice. I met her at Erik's house. Cindy, **whom** I met at Erik's house, is really nice.
whose	a possession	Dave is coming with us. You met his brother. Dave, **whose** brother you met, is coming with us.

A. Choose the correct word to complete the nonrestrictive clauses.

Example: Many friends celebrated my birthday, (who /(which)) was last week.

1. That yellow house, (whose / which) is now for sale, belongs to the Blooms.

2. Annika, (who / whose) dictionary I always use, is the smartest student in class.

3. Philippe, (who / whom) I just saw at the store, wants to go to Haiti.

4. The funniest kid in our class is Nicolas, (who / whom) sits in front of me.

5. That woman over there is Mrs. Li, (which / whose) dog is always running loose.

B. Combine the sentences with a nonrestrictive clause.

Example: I really need to find Caroline. I borrowed her pen.

I really need to find Caroline, whose pen I borrowed.

1. We're looking forward to the school dance. It is next week.

   _____

2. My uncle Pepe is getting married. You visited his restaurant a few times.

   _____

3. His girlfriend is named Donna. He knows her from college.

   _____

4. The math homework was very difficult. I didn't finish it.

   _____

Name _____ Date _____

● Writing Assignment
Short Story

Use with student book pages 244–245.

Use this chart to help you prewrite your short story.

1. First, think of a funny incident that happened to you. Briefly describe it. _____ _____ _____
2. Use metaphors to visualize the people, things, and events. _____ _____ _____

Person, thing, or event:	Metaphor:
the messy kitchen	a garbage dump
_____	_____
_____	_____

3. Imagine the sounds you heard during this event. Did you fall? Did something break? What other noises could you describe with an onomatopoeia? **Example:** _my bike brakes: My bike brakes screeched as I came to a sudden stop._ _____ _____ _____
4. You can enhance your story or make it funnier by using hyperbole. What details can you exaggerate for effect? **Example:** _I had a big plate of food. → My plate was piled to the ceiling with food._ _____ _____ _____

Name _____   Date _____

● **Writing Assignment**
Writing Support

Use with student book page 245.

> **Grammar: Interjections**
>
> An **interjection** expresses strong emotion. It usually is followed by an exclamation point (!).
> - An interjection is often used before another sentence that offers some additional explanation.
> - An interjection can also be used as a form of command.
> - An interjection can also come before a comma at the beginning of a sentence.
> - The word **oh** can be used as an interjection, either at the beginning or in the middle of a sentence.
>
> Here are some examples of interjections: **Cool, Hey, Hold on, Look, No, Oh, Oh no, Oops, Ouch, Ow, Stop, Wait, Wow**

A. Rewrite the sentences with the appropriate punctuation.

Example: Wow look at that old car! _____ *Wow! Look at that old car!* _____

1. Wait I'm coming with you. _____

2. Hey what was your name again? _____

3. Oops I spilled my drink on my homework! _____

4. Oh no I forgot about the English test today! _____

B. Write a sentence for each situation. Include an interjection.

Example: You find out that the jaceket you like is too expensive.
        Wow! This jacket is really expensive!

1. You hear a song you love on the radio; your friend is about to change the station.

   _____

2. You forgot to bring your English homework.

   _____

3. You are with your friend and you see something amazing.

   _____

4. The bus is about to drive away without you.

   _____

5. You just dropped a heavy book on your toe.

   _____

Name _____ Date _____

● Writing Assignment
Revising Activity

Use with student book page 245.

Read the paragraph from a student's short story.

1 My parents had the Kuo family over for dinner. My mother asked me to help. I piled the plates with mother's specialty and carried them.

A. Now rewrite paragraph 1 using at least four prepositional phrases and two appositives to make the sentences clearer and more descriptive. Try to use at least one prepositional phrase at the beginning of a sentence. Use your imagination to fill in the details.

_____

_____

_____

_____

Read the next paragraph.

2 I put Mr. Kuo's plate in front of him and smiled. I stepped to his left to serve Mrs. Kuo, but as I did, the plate slipped from my hand. (1) It hit the table and then slid into her lap. Everyone gasped. (2) "I'm so sorry!" I cried. (3) My face was bright red and hot. My mother and I ran to the kitchen to bring some wet towels. (4) We spent a long time wiping off Mrs. Kuo's yellow dress, but it still had sauce stains on it.

B. Rewrite paragraph 2. Enhance it with figurative language and exclamations. Try using an onomatopoeia in the Sentence 1, an exclamation in Sentence 2, a metaphor in Sentence 3, and a hyperbole in Sentence 4.

_____

_____

_____

_____

_____

_____

_____

_____

_____

Name _____ Date _____

● Writing Assignment
Editing Activity

Use with student book page 245.

A. Read this paragraph, fixing all errors in capitalization, spelling, punctuation, and word usage. Mark the mistakes using the editing marks on page 455 of your student book.

Mariana who is from Argentina joined our class at the beginning of the year. I really wanted to make a good impress on her, so I went over to her to try and start a converse. I asked her if she wanted to eat lunch with me on the cafeteria. I said, "I herd they're having apple cobbler for desert today." She replied, "Wow that sounds really good," but she looked on me like I was weird. Just then, I dropped my books! oh I was so embarrassed. As I bent over to pick them, our science teacher Mrs. Hart came out of the classroom. Mariana said to me, "Hey I need to go talk to Mrs. Hart," and she ran away. It may sound strange, but would you believe that Mariana is now my best friend?

B. Now rewrite the paragraph. Make the changes you marked above.

_____

_____

_____

_____

_____

_____

_____

_____

_____

_____

_____

_____

Name _____   Date _____

● Vocabulary From the Reading

Use with student book page 250.

> **Key Vocabulary**
> acknowledge   establish
> cherish   reflect
> enrich   symbolize

A. Write the Key Vocabulary word for each definition. The first one is done for you.

Example: <u>establish</u> to create; to start

Word	Definition
1. _____	to represent; to stand for
2. _____	to hold dear; to treasure
3. _____	to make better or fuller
4. _____	to recognize; to give notice to; to reward
5. _____	to think (about)

B. Complete each sentence with a Key Vocabulary word.

Example: My sister was so angry with me she did not even _____*acknowledge*_____ my presence at the dinner table.

1. I really _____ the valuable old books that Grandfather gave me.

2. The chef used cream and butter to _____ the soup.

3. The stars on the American flag _____ the fifty states.

4. Before you write your essay, _____ on this question.

5. They will _____ a new school in our neighborhood.

C. Use the Key Vocabulary words to describe a tradition or holiday you observe.

1. _____

2. _____

3. _____

Name _____ Date _____

● Reading Strategy

Use with student book page 251.

Tell Fact From Opinion

Telling facts from opinions will help you understand what you read. Remember that a fact must be supported by **proof.**

Academic Vocabulary for the Reading Strategy	
Word	**Explanation**
fact	something that can be proven
opinion	a personal view or idea
proof	evidence that shows something is true

Read the paragraph.

Benito Juárez, a Zapotec Indian from the state of Oaxaca, became the first full-blooded indigenous president of Mexico in 1858. Everyone in Mexico loves him. He was in exile from 1862 to 1867, during the French occupation. Then he continued serving until 1872, when he died in office. His birthday, March 21, is a national holiday in Mexico. It is celebrated on the third Monday in March. It's great because we don't have to go to school that day and many people don't have to go to work. I believe he was the greatest president in Mecico's history.

Now fill in this chart.

Fact	Opinion
Example: Benito Juárez, a Zapotec Indian from the state of Oaxaca, became the first full-blooded indigenous president of Mexico in 1858. 1. 2. 3.	1. 2. 3.

Name _____ Date _____

● **Text Genre**

Use with student book page 252.

Expository Text

Expository Text	
expert opinion	the opinion, or belief, of a person who knows a lot about the subject
place names	names of locations where important events happened

Read the passage.

1 Benito Juárez was born on March 21, 1806, in the Zapotec village of San Pablo Guelatao in the state of Oaxaca, Mexico. Although he was from a poor family and did not begin studying until he was twelve years old, he was eventually able to study law and become a judge; then he became the governor of Oaxaca in 1847. In 1848 he was exiled to New Orleans by the government of Santa Anna, but he returned to Mexico in 1855 and became the first full-blooded indigenous president of Mexico in 1858. He served for fourteen years until 1872, when he died of a heart attack at the National Palace in Mexico City.

2 Many consider Juárez to be one of the most important figures in Mexican history, inspired by his rise from poverty to political greatness. In her booklet *Juárez el Republicano,* historian Josefina Zoraida Vázquez describes Juárez as "an extraordinary case in history, since although he was born in the heart of an isolated and monolingual ethnic group in the Oaxacan mountains and of humble origins," he was able to rise to the highest position in the country.

Complete the chart and answer the question.

Place Name	Event	Date
San Pablo Guelatao, Oaxaca		

Was there an expert opinion in this reading? If so, whose? _____

_____

Name _____ Date _____

● Reading Comprehension

Use with student book page 261.

Academic Vocabulary for the Reading Comprehension Questions	
classify	to divide things into groups so that similar things are in the same group

A. **Retell the story.** Summarize the theme of each section.

Introduction: _____

_____

Celebration in Los Angeles: _____

_____

The Meaning of Cinco de Mayo: _____

_____

Different Meanings to Different People: _____

_____

Celebrate Cinco de Mayo: _____

_____

B. **Write your response.** Classify the following as a fact or an opinion: "Cinco de Mayo celebrations in the U.S. miss the true meaning of the holiday." Do you agree or disagree? Explain.

_____

_____

_____

C. **Assess the reading strategy.** Now you have practiced distinguishing facts from opinions. How does this help you understand the text?

_____

_____

_____

Name _____ Date _____

● **Text Element**

Use with student book page 261.

Author's Perspective

Every author has opinions and attitudes about the subjects he or she describes or writes about. These opinions and attitudes are the author's perspective. When you read, ask the following questions to discover the author's perspective:

1. Does the author describe his or her feelings about the subject? What are they?
2. What do you know about the author's background? Why do you think the author chose to write about the subject he or she did?
3. What kinds of words does the author use? What can the author's words tell you about his or her perspective?

Read the sentences in a student's paper about Halloween traditions at his school. What does each sentence tell you about the author's perspective? Fill in the chart.

(1) Every October, students look forward to Halloween; this day is less serious than other days, and there is a feeling of fun in the air. (2) Several years ago, students and teachers could come to school in their costumes and go through the whole day in them; now, the students can only put their costumes on at the end of the day. (3) Still, everyone is excited about the afternoon parade and Halloween party in the gym. (4) There is usually a complex haunted-house area, created by some students with the help of parents and teachers to make it more realistic and frightening. (5) At the end, there is one costume contest for students and one for teachers—and the students get the chance to vote for the best teacher's costume!

Sentence	Author's Perspective
1	
2	
3	
4	
5	

Name _____   Date _____

● Vocabulary From the Reading

Use with student book page 262.

> **Key Vocabulary**
>
> entangled   snare
> glisten   stomp
> hum

A. Write the correct letter for the underlined Key Vocabulary word.

Example: ___C___ Grandmother <u>hummed</u> a traditional song.

   a. sang loudly   b. played on a guitar   c. sang with closed lips

1. _____ The ice <u>glistened</u> in the sun.

   a. glittered   b. melted   c. became slippery and dangerous

2. _____ The hunter <u>snared</u> a rabbit.

   a. saw   b. trapped, caught   c. chased, ran after

3. _____ Teresa <u>stomped</u> on the floor.

   a. stepped forcefully   b. fell down   c. danced gracefully

4. _____ The ribbons were <u>entangled</u> in Sara's hair.

   a. tied neatly   b. clipped, pinned   c. wrapped, twisted

B. Complete each sentence using Key Vocabulary words. Be sure to use the correct form of the word.

Example: The boy _____*stomped*_____ on the floor.

1. The fishermen _____ tuna in their nets.

2. That's a lovely melody you are _____.

3. Her diamond ring _____ in the bright light.

4. Don't _____ when you walk; the neighbors can hear you!

5. The rope was _____ into a knot.

C. Use three of the Key Vocabulary words in sentences.

1. _____

2. _____

3. _____

Name _____ Date _____

● Reading Strategy

Use with student book page 263.

Ask Questions

> **Asking questions** will help you understand what happens in a story. You should ask questions before, during, and after reading.

A. Before you read the story below, ask two questions about it. Look for the answers as you read.

Question:	Does Jackie ever smile?
Answer:	

Grumpy Little Jackie

Jackie was a grumpy eleven-year-old girl. She didn't speak to her relatives when they came to visit, she didn't share things with her brothers and sisters, and she never said "thank you" when someone gave her a present.

B. Now that you have read the first paragraph, ask two questions you have about the story before you continue. Look for the answers as you read.

Question:	_____?
Answer:	
Question:	_____?
Answer:	

One year on Jackie's birthday, her family decided to teach her a lesson. Everyone arrived at the house for a party, but no one said "hello" to Jackie and no one gave her a present. They did not talk to her and they did not sing to her. Jackie angrily asked, "Why aren't you talking to me? Why aren't you singing to me? This is my party! Where are my presents?" One aunt looked at her and said, "I didn't bring a present because you never seem thankful." Jackie left the room in tears. The next day, everyone returned with presents and smiles. "Surprise!" they all said as Jackie came into the room. She was smiling, too.

C. Now that you finished the story, ask another question.

Question:	_____?

Name _____ Date _____

● Text Genre

Use with student book page 263.

Legend: Native American Legend

Native American Legend	
personification of animals	animal characters who speak and act like people
moral	lesson based on ideas about what is right or wrong

Read this legend. Then answer the questions that follow.

Iktomi and the Muskrat

1 Iktomi was a spirit who didn't have many friends because of his selfish ways. One day, he was sitting beside a lake eating a pot of fish soup when he heard a voice in the grass say, "Hello, my friend!" Iktomi turned to see a wet muskrat* who had just come out of the lake.

2 "Hello!" Iktomi replied. The muskrat smiled, waiting for Iktomi to offer him some food, which was the proper etiquette. Iktomi just sat rudely and hummed. Finally, Iktomi said, "Let's run a race to the other side of the lake. If I win, I won't have to share it with you. If you win, you can have half of it." The muskrat replied, "but you are a much faster runner than I am." Iktomi finally agreed to run the race with a heavy stone on his back, and they began.

3 After several minutes, Iktomi looked across the lake. He didn't see any sign of the muskrat. "Oh no!" he thought, "Did the muskrat run faster than I?" He threw off the stone and ran to where the pot of soup was. He heard a voice laughing above him. The muskrat was sitting up in a tree eating the soup. He had swum across the lake instead of running! Iktomi called to him, "Oh, my friend, please share your food with me!" He opened his mouth, but the muskrat only dropped a fish bone on his head. The muskrat laughed and said, "Next time you have a visitor, invite him to share your food!"

1. Who is the animal character in the story? Describe him. _____

_____

_____

2. What is the moral of the story? Who learns the lesson? _____

_____

_____

_____
*a rodent who lives in the water, similar to a beaver

● Reading Comprehension

Use with student book page 267.

A. **Retell the story.** In your own words, summarize the "Legend of the Dreamcatcher."

_____

_____

_____

_____

_____

_____

_____

B. **Write your response.** Did you enjoy the legend? Why or why not?

_____

_____

_____

_____

_____

C. **Assess the reading strategy.** How did asking questions before, during, and after the reading help enhance your understanding?

_____

_____

_____

_____

_____

Name _____ Date _____

● Spelling
Checking Spelling with a Dictionary

Use with student book page 267.

When you are not sure how a word is spelled, look it up in a dictionary.

- Start by flipping to the correct section for the first letter of the word. If you are not sure what letter the word starts with, think of how the word sounds.

f (foam)	g (general)	c (cent)	c (canoe)
ph (phone)	j (jig)	s (sent), ps (psyche)	k (kayak)

- Then move on to the next letters in the word. Try different letters. If you have trouble, try different letter combinations.

ch (reach)	sh (washing)	ge (age)	ee (seem)
tch (catch)	ci, sci (conscious), ti (action)	dge (edge)	ea (seam), ie (believe)

- Remember that some letters are silent (*reign, fight, doubt*).
- Check the definition to make sure you have the right word. Many words sound alike but mean different things (**cent** / **sent** / **scent**).

Use a dictionary to check the spelling of the underlined words in the following sentences. Correct the words.

                                       nations   Chippewa   Algonsuin

Example: Two Native American ~~nacions~~ are the ~~Chipewa~~, and the ~~Algonkouin~~.

1. Cinse I was a child, I have apresciated their glorius folclorick traditions.

2. My mother hung a majical charm over my cradel.

3. The archduque Maximilian was appointed as emporer of Mexico in 1864.

4. Mexico fought for its soverinty, or freedom from forign rule.

5. Is our fisical education class cansiled because the teatcher is sic?

6. The rost beef gave off a delishus cent.

● Writing Conventions
Punctuation: Dialogue

Use with student book page 267.

Quotation marks (" ") appear before and after the exact words spoken by a character. If dialogue appears at the beginning of a sentence, place a comma (,) at the end of the line spoken by the character: "Wait**,**" said the grandmother.

If the dialogue is a question or an exclamation, keep the original punctuation:
   "Nokomis-iya**!**" he shouted.
   "Why do you protect the spider**?**" asked the little boy.

If the dialogue is at the end of the sentence, a comma should come before it, and the first letter should be capitalized: He said to her, **"F**or many days you have watched me spin and weave my web."

If the dialogue is at the beginning *and* end of a sentence, use commas to separate the spoken words from the rest of the sentence. Do not capitalize the first word of the second quote: "No-keegwa," the old lady whispered, **"d**on't hurt him."

A.   Edit the following lines. Add the necessary punctuation. Use editing marks.

Example: " Come on'" she said '"there's a Dairy Queen down the street."
             ^   ^   ^   ^

1. Do try some of the celery, Mrs. Lin she said.

2. Tilt your plate whispered my mother.

3. Wait one minute I said and I'll be right out.

B.   Rewrite these sentences, fixing the errors of punctuation and capitalization.

Example: you must not hurt the spider said the grandmother.

   "You must not hurt the spider," said the grandmother.

1. "It's not bad! She whispered."

   _____

2. "oh" sighed Mrs. Gleason "This food is wonderful"!

   _____

3. The waiter leaned in and said "tonight's special is ***pâté en croute.***

   _____

Name _____ Date _____

● Vocabulary Development

Use with student book page 269.

Foreign Words and Phrases

Many words and phrases from other languages are used in the English language. Even though these words are commonly understood among English speakers, they are considered **foreign**. Foreign means being from another language, country, or culture.

Read the sentences. Then match each word or phrase with the correct definition.

- Antonio is feeling **angst** about his first day of junior high school.
- Mimi is a baseball **aficionado.**
- Our science teacher is a **bona fide** expert on dinosaurs.
- Samuel Clemens's **nom de plume** was Mark Twain.
- We ate **crêpes** with Hannah at the **café.**
- The **chef** prepared six different types of **pasta** for the **buffet.**

Example: __f__ angst (German)

1. _____ aficionado (Spanish)

  a. a thin pancake

2. _____ bona fide (Latin)

  b. a coffee shop; coffeehouse

3. _____ nom de plume (French)

  c. a professional cook

4. _____ crêpe (French)

  d. dough made from flour and water, formed into various shapes (e.g. spaghetti, macaroni)

5. _____ café (French)

  e. authentic; real

6. _____ chef (French)

  f. anxiety; nervousness; fear

7. _____ pasta (Italian)

  g. an informal dinner spread out on a table; guests serve themselves

8. _____ buffet (French)

  h. a fan; follower

  i. pen name

Name _____ Date _____

● Grammar
Use with student book page 270.
Indefinite Pronouns

Indefinite pronouns refer to unspecified people or things. Most indefinite pronouns are singular and take singular verbs.

Indefinite Pronouns	
singular pronouns	**sentence**
another, either, much, one, anybody, everybody, neither, other, anyone, everyone, nobody, somebody, anything, everything, no one, someone, each, little, nothing, something	**Everyone** <u>has</u> a chance to go. **Each** of the men <u>wants</u> to win. **Nobody** hears the door slam.
plural pronouns	**sentence**
both, few, many, several	**Both** seem like good choices. **Many** of the students are in the classroom.

Some indefinite pronouns are either singular or plural and take either singular or plural verbs, depending on what the indefinite pronoun refers to.

singular or plural pronouns	sentence
all, any, most, none, some	**All** of the snow has melted. **All** of the students are reading. **Some** of the guests eat with chopsticks. **Some** of the food is on the table.

Circle the correct indefinite pronoun or verb to complete each sentence.

Example: ((Each) / All) of the students does the homework.

1. All of the cookies (is / are) burnt.

2. Everybody (was / were) in class today.

3. I like lasagna and macaroni. (Both / Each) are delicious.

4. Many (are / is) interested in the show, but (few / no one) is buying tickets.

5. None of my homework (require / requires) a textbook today.

6. I can't decide between the kittens. (Both / Each) are cute.

7. (Someone / Anyone) is calling my cell phone.

Name _____   Date _____

● **Grammar**   *Use with student book page 271.*

Classifying Sentences by Purpose

Sentence	Purpose	Examples
interrogative	to ask a question	Was he right after all?
declarative	to make a statement	The decision angered her parents.
exclamatory	to express a strong feeling	Oh, I just made it!
imperative	to give an order	Tell me what you think about the poem. Don't forget your house keys!

A.   Fill in the letter for the correct sentence type.

Example: ___*e*___ How are you?

1. _____ The book is really interesting.   a. imperative and exclamatory

2. _____ What do you think about the book?   b. declarative

3. _____ Read the last chapter carefully.   c. exclamatory

4. _____ I love the book!   d. imperative

5. _____ Give me my book back! ·   e. interrogative

B.   Rewrite each sentence as a different type of sentence.

Example: Are we leaving now? (declarative) ___We are leaving now.___

1. I want you to clean your room. (imperative) _____

2. He is happy. (interrogative) _____

3. I like your jacket. (exclamatory) _____

4. Don't cross the street without looking! (declarative) _____

C.   There is a new student in your English class. Write four sentences directed to the new student. Use one of each type of sentence from the chart above. Label each one.

Example: ___Welcome to the class! (exclamatory)___

1. _____

2. _____

3. _____

4. _____

Name _____ Date _____

● Grammar Expansion
Using Indefinite Pronouns: Avoiding Double Negatives

Be sure to use the correct indefinite pronoun depending on the sentence type and the verb form you are using.

Incorrect: There **isn't nothing** on the table.
Correct: There **is nothing** on the table. OR There **isn't anything** on the table.

Questions	Negative Verbs	Affirmative Verbs
some, someone, somebody, something; any, anyone, anybody, anything	any, anyone, anybody, anything	some, someone, somebody, something; none, no one, nobody, nothing
Do you have **any** money?	No, I don't have **any**.	Yes, I have **some**. No, I have **none**.
Did you see **anyone** in the classroom?	No, I didn't see **anybody**.	Yes, I saw **someone**. No, I saw **nobody**.
Do you want **something**?	No, I don't want **anything**.	Yes, I want **something**. No, I want **nothing**.

A. Circle the correct indefinite pronoun to complete each statement.

Example: Would you like (none /(some)) of this orange juice?

1. I don't like (none / any) of the clothes in this store.

2. I didn't bring (nothing / anything) today for lunch.

3. Doesn't (nobody / anybody) have $5.00 I can borrow?

4. I don't see (somebody / anybody) on the school bus yet.

5. There isn't (anyone / no one) from Armenia in my English class.

6. Raquel doesn't know (anyone / no one) in her English class.

B. Answer the following **yes** / **no** questions, using an indefinite pronoun in each answer. Give true answers.

Example: Is there anything on your desk? _Yes, there is something on my desk._

1. Do you have any money in your pocket? _____

2. Do you want something to eat right now? _____

3. Did your friends tell you anything interesting yesterday? _____

4. Did you talk to anyone on the phone yesterday? _____

5. Did you have any milk this morning at breakfast? _____

Name _____ Date _____

● Grammar Expansion
Tag Questions

A tag question is an interrogative statement tagged onto the end of a declarative statement. Use a tag question when you want to get confirmation or agreement from someone. Here is how tag questions are formed:

Original Statement (Verb is underlined.)	"Opposite" Verb Form	Statement with Tag Question (Pronoun replaces subject.)
I am your brother.	aren't	I am your brother, aren't I?
I'm not the best.	am	I'm not the best, am I?
Kendra is a nice person.	isn't	Kendra is a nice person, isn't she?
They aren't going to Peru.	are	They aren't going to Peru, are they?
Ricardo lives there.	doesn't (live)	Ricardo lives there, doesn't he?
Ricardo doesn't have a dog.	does (have)	Ricardo doesn't have a dog, does he?
You were there.	weren't	You were there, weren't you?
I wasn't acting rude.	was	I wasn't acting rude, was I?
You ate lunch.	didn't (eat)	You ate lunch, didn't you?
You didn't eat my apple.	did (eat)	You didn't eat my apple, did you?

Note: When talking about oneself, **aren't I?** is most commonly used. In very formal situations, the tag question **am I not?** can be used.

A. Correct the errors in the following tag questions.

Example: We don't have a test today, ~~aren't~~ we?
                                              ^do

1. You're not hungry again, aren't you?

2. I'm not wrong, are I?

3. We have enough money, do we?

B. Complete these sentences with the correct tag question.

Example: You aren't sleeping yet, _____are you_____?

1. Bobby doesn't have the flu, _____?

2. The Cinco de Mayo party was fun, _____?

3. Your mother has a blue car, _____?

4. These books aren't yours, _____?

Name _____ Date _____

● Writing Assignment
Write an Informative Essay

Use with student book pages 272–273.

A. First, brainstorm a list of holidays that you celebrate. Which ones are more interesting or fun? Which ones might your classmates want to learn more about? Decide which holiday you want to write about and circle it.

Holidays I Celebrate	
_____	_____
_____	_____
_____	_____

B. Use this chart to help you fill in details about the holiday.

Who?	
What?	
When?	
Where?	
Why?	
How long?	

Name _____ Date _____

● Writing Assignment

Use with student book page 273.

Writing Support

Mechanics: Sentence Punctuation

- Use a period at the end of declarative statements.
    It is my favorite holiday.

- Use an exclamation point at the end of exclamatory sentences.
    I can't believe it's already here!

- Use a question mark at the end of interrogative sentences.
    When is that holiday celebrated?

- You may use a period or an exclamation point at the end of imperative sentences, depending on how much emotion is being used.
    Don't forget to decorate.
    Open your present now!

A. Add the most appropriate punctuation at the end of each sentence.

Example: Do you have to go to school on Columbus Day __?__

1. Thanksgiving is celebrated on the fourth Thursday in November _____

2. What do Americans do on Flag Day _____

3. I can't wait until the 4ᵗʰ of July _____

4. To celebrate Halloween, put on a funny or scary costume _____

B. Write a sentence for each situation. Use an appropriate sentence type.

Example: You just learned that you are getting out of school early today because tomorrow is Thanksgiving.

    It's great that we are getting out of school early today!

1. You want to tell someone what your favorite holiday is.

    _____

2. You want to find out what someone else's favorite holiday is.

    _____

3. You are very happy about a birthday present you received.

    _____

Name _____ Date _____

● **Writing Assignment**
Revising Activity

Use with student book page 273.

Read over your essay carefully. Answer the following questions.

1. Did you write three paragraphs? Are they organized, and do the sentences in each paragraph support the main idea? To check, write the main idea of each paragraph below. Then reread your supporting statements and remove or revise any that don't fit.

   First paragraph: _____

   Second paragraph: _____

   Third paragraph: _____

2. Does your essay contain correct information? Did you use sources like encyclopedias or history books to find information about the holiday's origins? Go back to your essay and recheck the facts against a reliable source.

   Fact 1: _____

   Source: _____

   Fact 2: _____

   Source: _____

   Fact 3: _____

   Source: _____

3. Does your essay use at least two different sentence types? If so, which ones?

   _____

   If not, add a second type of sentence. Try writing it here first:

   _____

4. Did you use indefinite pronouns? If so, which ones?

   _____

   If not, add or revise a sentence to include indefinite pronouns:

   _____

Name _____ Date _____

● Writing Assignment

Use with student book page 273.

Editing Activity

A. Read this paragraph. Use editing marks to correct mistakes in capitalization, spelling, punctuation, and word usage. Mark the mistakes using the editing marks on page 455 of your student book.

    Every year on Valentine's Day, everyone bring cards to class to give to each classmates? Any students buy a box of cards at the store, but others make their own cards. Anybody always bring in little candy hearts that say be mine. or you're great! on them; but I don't usually eat none because they aren't very good. Last year I made my own Valentine cards for the class. Everyone loved them? Both the students came up to me and said you didn't make these yourself, didn't you or these are so cool They couldn't believe I didn't buy them in the store

B. Now rewrite the paragraph with your corrections.

_____

_____

_____

_____

_____

_____

_____

_____

_____

_____

_____

_____

Name _____ Date _____

● Vocabulary From the Reading

Use with student book page 290.

> **Key Vocabulary**
>
> accomplish   escort
> destination   stunned
> emphasize

A. Write the Key Vocabulary word for each definition.

Example: _emphasize_ to put special importance on something

Word	Definition
1. _____	a person who accompanies someone
2. _____	to surprise; to shock; to make speechless
3. _____	final goal; place where someone is going
4. _____	to achieve; to finish; to do

B. Fill in the correct Key Vocabulary word to complete each sentence. Be sure to use the correct form of the word.

Example: I spent two hours on my project, and I ___accomplished___ a lot.

1. The movie star never goes out alone; she always has an _____.

2. I was _____ when I heard I won first prize in the essay contest.

3. Our English teacher likes to _____ the importance of reading.

4. We stopped in Miami, but our final _____ was Santo Domingo.

C. Answer the questions.

1. When was the last time you felt stunned? Why?

_____

2. What is something you have accomplished recently?

_____

3. When was the last time you traveled? What was your destination?

_____

Name _____ Date _____

● Reading Strategy

Use with student book page 291.

Describe Mental Images

Many stories include words that help you to **describe mental images** as you read. When you create an image of the details you read about, it helps you to understand and remember what you have read.

Describing mental images allows readers to use all of their senses to imagine the details in a story. You can create an image of how something sounds, smells, feels, or even tastes.

Academic Vocabulary for the Reading Strategy	
Word	**Explanation**
image	a mental picture of someone or something

Read the paragraph. As you read, make mental images of the characters and setting. Complete the chart. In the left-hand column, write the vivid details from the story. In the right-hand column, describe the image each detail helped you visualize.

There we were—40 frightened students sitting in the principal's small office, waiting for him to arrive. He had summoned us all there after we returned from our field trip. We didn't know what was going to happen to us. Some students did not behave perfectly at the museum, but we didn't think anyone deserved to go to the principal's office. As we waited for Mr. Wells to arrive, the only sound in the room was the hiss and gurgle of the coffeemaker as it sputtered out the principal's afternoon pot of coffee. Finally, we heard the *clomp-clomp-clomp* of Mr. Wells's shoes approaching the door. On our side of the door, it was dead quiet.

Detail from the Story	Image
40 frightened students huddled into the principal's small office	A group of students with scared looks on their faces, very quietly sitting and standing very close to each other, exchanging worried looks

Name _____ Date _____

● **Text Genre**

Use with student book page 292.

Novel

Novel	
narrator	the character or voice that tells a story
setting	where and when a story takes place
dialogue	the words that the characters speak; the words are in quotation marks (" ")

Read the excerpt from a story. Then answer the questions below it.

1. You all probably think of me, the principal, as someone to fear. You probably think I am someone with great power who cannot be harmed. But I want to tell you a story that might make you think differently about me.

2. When I was your age, sitting in one of those very same chairs at one of those very same desks, I was just like you. I was sent to the principal's office one afternoon for writing my name on my desk. I laughed with my friends during class. Sometimes I didn't pay attention; sometimes I threw a paper airplane.

3. One day Mr. Reiser came to class and said, "Mr. Buckley, the principal wants to see you." I laughed and said, "Mr. Buckley? He must want to give me an award." But Mr. Reiser didn't laugh. I knew I was in trouble.

1. Who is the narrator?

   _____

2. What is the setting of the story the narrator tells?

   _____

   _____

3. What does the narrator say in the dialogue?

   _____

   _____

Name _____ Date _____

● Reading Comprehension

Use with student book page 303.

Academic Vocabulary for the Reading Comprehension Questions		
Word	Explanation	
attitude	an opinion or way of thinking	
reveal	to uncover something that is hidden or secret	

A. Retell the story. In your own words, retell the story *Code Talker*.

_____

_____

_____

_____

_____

B. Write your response. What was the author's attitude toward his mission during the war? In your opinion, which line or paragraph from the text best reveals this attitude?

_____

_____

_____

C. Assess the reading strategy. As you read, you were asked to make mental images of the setting, characters, and action. How did mental images help you understand the story?

_____

_____

_____

Name _____ Date _____

● Literary Element

Use with student book page 303.

Idiom

> An **idiom** is an expression or phrase that does not have the same meaning as its individual words. In an idiom, the words have a different meaning.

A. The sentences contain idioms. Choose the best definition for each idiom.

Example: __b__ I couldn't <u>make heads or tails of</u> the note she wrote.

      a. find   b. read, understand   c. answer

1. _____ Can you <u>keep an eye on</u> my things for a minute? I'll be right back.
   a. hide   b. help carry   c. watch

2. _____ I didn't call you for any particular reason; I just wanted to <u>shoot the breeze</u>.
   a. chat   b. relax   c. enjoy the outdoors

3. _____ School is canceled today? I don't believe it. You're <u>pulling my leg</u>!
   a. telling the truth   b. bothering me   c. joking

4. _____ I joined the math team last week, but it is harder than I thought it would be. I think I might be <u>in over my head</u>.
   a. in a situation   b. in a situation   c. advancing upward
      that is too difficult   that is educational

5. _____ The homework last night was <u>a piece of cake</u>; I finished it in 15 minutes!
   a. difficult   b. easy   c. fun

B. Write the appropriate idiom to complete each sentence. Choose from these six idioms: **dry run, set foot in, breathe a word, hit the sack, top drawer,** and **round up.**

Example: The fire drill was just a _____*dry run*_____ to teach us what to do in a real emergency.

1. The boys were scared, and they refused to _____ the old, abandoned garage.

2. Please, do not _____ of this to anyone! It is a secret!

3. Jim was exhausted. He just wanted to go home and _____.

Name _____   Date _____

● Vocabulary From the Reading

Use with student book page 304.

> **Key Vocabulary**
>
> corps   mission
> engage   standard
> invest

A. Match each Key Vocabulary word to its definition.

Example: ___*c*___ corps

1. _____ standard

2. _____ invest

3. _____ mission

4. _____ engage

a. task; goal

b. to involve; to hold the attention of; to keep busy

c. an organized group

d. something established as a model or example

e. to commit (resources, money) to something in order to get something back in the future

B. Complete each sentence with one of the Key Vocabulary words. Be sure to use the correct form of the word.

Example: The topic in science class really ____*engaged*____ the students.

1. Vanessa's essay was so good, the teacher displayed it as a _____ for the class.

2. Our drum and bugle _____ marched in the school parade.

3. My main _____ today is to find the perfect birthday present for my mother.

4. My father _____ all his money in stocks and bonds.

5. My family is very _____ in traditional Greek customs.

● Reading Strategy
Analyze Text Evidence

Use with student book page 305.

> When you **analyze text evidence**, you look within the reading for evidence, or proof, that supports a point. Text evidence can be in the form of facts, details, quotes, or even pictures. Often, text evidence answers questions that come up as you read.

Read the paragraph from a company's Web site. In the charts below, fill in three points or messages that the company wants to communicate about itself. Then find three pieces of evidence in the text to support each point or message.

We produce the most intelligent electronic games in the world. We hire only the best engineers, we test all our products, and we offer the newest technology available. Our games are not only exciting, but also educational because kids must use intelligence to solve problems. To play our games, kids must learn to make good decisions and develop critical-thinking skills. Most importantly, every game is kid-tested. First, we ask kids what games they like. Then we ask them how to make the games. Finally, we let them play our games, so we know that they love our products!

Point or Message 1:

We produce the most intelligent electronic games in the world.

→

Text Evidence:

1. best software engineers

2. _____

3. _____

Point or Message 2:

_____

_____

_____

→

Text Evidence:

1. _____

2. _____

3. _____

Point or Message 3:

_____

_____

_____

→

Text Evidence:

1. _____

2. _____

3. _____

Name _____ Date _____

● Text Genre

Use with student book page 305.

Informational Text

Brochure	
bullets	dots or small symbols used to create lists
headings	boldfaced words or phrases used to introduce sections of material
testimonials	direct quotes from people who share positive experiences with the company or product

Read the brochure below. Circle and label each of the features from the chart above.

"English Action has given me the chance to get a better job and improve the life of my family. Thanks!" —Edmundo Villaverde, age 34, El Salvador, English Action trainee

English Action: Action for the Community

Since 2000, English Action has been recruiting and training local volunteers to tutor recent immigrants and refugees. Since then, more than 120 volunteers have helped hundreds of immigrants in the community!

Our Mission Statement

English Action seeks to achieve the following:
- to offer tutoring in English and office skills to those who need them
- to improve the lives of immigrants and refugees
- to provide an opportunity for local residents to give back to their community

What People Are Saying
- "Becoming an English Action tutor was the best thing I ever did!" —Martha Knowles, age 21, English Action volunteer
- "My tutor was so friendly and helpful. I learned so much, so fast!" —Svetlana Akilov, age 19, Russia, English Action student
- "I was proud to be able to use my years of office experience to help someone learn English for business." —Fred Williams, age 57, English Action volunteer

---

Name _____ Date _____

● **Reading Comprehension**   *Use with student book page 309.*

A. **Retell the story.** How did City Year get started? What are some of the services offered by City Year? What are the benefits for the volunteers?

_____

_____

_____

_____

_____

B. **Write your response.** What kinds of services do you think City Year could offer in your community? What would you want to do as a City Year volunteer?

_____

_____

_____

_____

_____

C. **Assess the reading strategy.** As you read, you were asked to analyze the text evidence. Did it help you to identify the main messages and the evidence that supports them? How?

_____

_____

_____

_____

_____

Name _____ Date _____

● **Spelling**

Use with student book page 309.

The Combination *ph*

In many words and names in English, the combination **ph** is used to show an **f** sound.

Philip telegra**ph** am**ph**ibious

A. Circle all examples of the **f** sound in the following words. Some of the words do not have an **f** sound in them.

Example: ⓕight

1. photograph
2. emphasize
3. proof
4. Joseph

5. telephone
6. printed
7. different
8. useful

9. paragraph
10. platoon
11. elephant
12. battlefield

B. Correct the spelling errors in the following sentences.

                                   perfectly
Example: We spoke the language ⌃perphectly.

1. Is there a telefone in the farmacy?

2. The Navajo code helped the phighters on the battlephield.

3. The Navajo phlatoon had to use dipherent types of equipment, such as the telegraf.

4. Did you see the fotograf of Josef Bruchac?

5. My grandphather lives on a pharm.

C. Write four sentences using words that contain the combination **ph.**

1. _____

2. _____

3. _____

4. _____

● Writing Conventions
Punctuation: Using Bulleted Lists

Use with student book page 309.

When you are writing a business letter, informational brochure, or poster, a bulleted list helps you show lists of information more clearly.

Sentence Form	A survey of City Year **alumni** found that 95% indicated that they made an important difference in someone's life while at City Year, and 88% indicated that they often worked with people from different backgrounds while at City Year.
Bulleted List	A survey of City Year **alumni** found that • 95% of participants felt that they made an important difference in someone's life while at City Year • 88% of participants often worked with people from different backgrounds while at City Year

Rewrite the sentences as bulleted lists. Use the chart above as a model.

1. To apply, you need to be a student between the ages 10 and 15, to have a grade average of C or above, and to get permission from your parents.

   _____

   _____

   _____

2. With my letter I am including my application, a photo, a permission letter from my parents, and the program fee of $150.

   _____

   _____

   _____

3. If you volunteer in your community, you will learn a lot, develop new skills, meet new and different people, and make a difference in people's lives.

   _____

   _____

   _____

Name _____ Date _____

● Vocabulary Development

Use with student book page 311.

Using a Dictionary and a Thesaurus

A **dictionary** provides definitions of words; most dictionaries also provide other information, such as a word's part of speech and etymology (word origin). A **thesaurus** provides synonyms, or words that are similar in meaning. Together, these tools can help you to choose the most effective words.

Look at this dictionary entry:
  academy (ə kadʹə mē) *n.* (pl. -ies) **1** a school, or place of study or training [from Greek Akadēmos, the Greek mythological hero]

Look at this entry from a thesaurus:
  academy (noun) school, college, university, boarding school, institute

A. Use both a dictionary and a thesaurus to complete the following chart.

word	pronunciation	part of speech	definition	etymology	synonyms
gift	/gift/	n.			
problem					
punish					
nickname					

B. Replace each underlined word with a more effective word from a thesaurus. Check the definition of the new word in a dictionary to make sure it carries the correct meaning.

Example: Mrs. Vieira is a̲ ̲n̲i̲c̲e̲ woman.
                       ‸ *an amiable*

1. The volunteer program is good for the community.

2. You will have to do many tasks as a volunteer.

3. There are many ways you can help.

200

Name _____ Date _____

● Grammar
Use with student book pages 312–313.

Present Perfect, Past Perfect, and Future Perfect Tenses

Use the **present perfect tense** to describe an action that occurred in the past and continues to occur in the present. You can also use the present perfect tense to describe an action that has happened in an unspecified time in the past.

Present Perfect Tense			
subject	auxiliary verb	main verb	
I / You / We / They	have	lived	here for one year.
He / She / It	has		

Use the **past perfect tense** to describe an action that was completed in the past before another action.

Past Perfect Tense			
subject	auxiliary verb	main verb	
I / You / We / They	had	worked	for the company for two years when we met.
He / She / It	had		

Use **future perfect tense** to describe action that will take place in the future before another event occurs.

Future Perfect Tense			
subject	auxiliary verb	main verb	
I / You / We / They	will have	graduated	high school by next summer.
He / She / It	will have		

Name _____ Date _____

A. Circle the correct verb form to complete each sentence.

Example: By next June, we (had / have /(will have)) completed our studies.

1. I (will have / had / have) heard of James Brown before you played me some of his music.

2. We (have / had / will have) never seen an Indian movie. Will you show us one?

3. I am still working on my composition, but I (have / will have / had) finished it by the time you arrive.

4. Sam (has / will have / had) already gone to bed when we called his house.

B. Fill in the blank with the present, past, or future perfect tense.

Example: Vitas invited me to lunch, but I _____had eaten_____ (eat) already.

1. Tim _____ (arrive) home by the time I get there this afternoon.

2. We _____ (live) at this address for two years now.

3. When Stacy went to get a glass of milk, she discovered that her mother

   _____ (use) it all to make tapioca pudding.

4. By 9:00 tonight, I _____ (learn) fifteen new words in English.

5. You _____ (watch) this movie before, right?

6. Mario _____ (try) African food only once before he met Yvette's family.

C. Answer the questions.

1. What have you learned this week in science class?

   _____

2. What had you learned before that?

   _____

3. Name three things that you will have done by next Saturday morning.

   _____

Name _____ Date _____

● Grammar Expansion

Yes / No Questions and Negative Statements in the Present and Past Perfect Tenses

Yes / No Questions				
tense	*have / had*	subject	past participle	
Present Perfect	Have	I / you / we / they	seen	the movie?
	Has	he / she / it		
Past Perfect	Had	I / you / we / they he / she / it		

Negative Statements				
tense	subject	*have not* *had not*	past participle	
Present Perfect	I / You / We / They	have not	seen	the movie.
	He / She / It	has not		
Past Perfect	I / You / We / They He / She / It	had not		

Note: Use the word **yet** in questions or to tell about things that have not happened but will or might happen:

Have you eaten lunch yet?

My friends invited me to play basketball, but I had not finished my homework yet.

A. Complete the question or the answer with the present or past perfect.

Example: Have you seen the original *Star Wars* trilogy?

No, _I have not seen_ it.

1. Has Mike been to Mexico? No, _____ to Mexico.

2. _____ Marc before yesterday? No, I had not called him before yesterday.

3. Have you finished your homework yet? No, _____ it yet.

4. _____ the news about Elise? No, I had not heard it before.

B. Use the present and past perfect to write two sentences about things you have not done yet and things that you had not done until recently.

1. _____

2. _____

Name _____ Date _____

● Grammar Expansion

Yes / No Questions and Negative Statements in the Future Perfect Tense

Yes / No Questions				
will	subject	*have*	past participle	
Will	I she / he / it / we / you / they	have	eaten	dinner by 5:00?

Negative Statements			
subject	*Will not have*	past participle	
I She / He / It / We / You / They	Will not have	eaten	dinner by 5:00.

A. Unscramble the following sentences and questions. Capitalize the first letter.

Example: homework / not / will / 3:00 / have / I / finished / all / my / by / .

<u>I will not have finished all my homework by 3:00.</u>

1. tomorrow / by / she / have / will / returned / trip / her / from / ?

   _____

2. we / learned / will / English / perfect / have / end / by / year / the / of / the / ?

   _____

3. not / enough / you / saved / by / month / money / will / next / have / .

   _____

4. ends / have / the / when / dinner / not / will / eaten / we / food / all / the / .

   _____

B. Write two questions for your friends using the future perfect tense. Then write two negative sentences about yourself in the future perfect.

Example: <u>Will you have finished visiting your grandmother by 6:00 on Friday?</u>

1. _____

2. _____

3. _____

4. _____

● Writing Assignment

Business Letter Asking for Information

Use this chart to help you organize your thoughts before you write your letter.

Paragraph 1

Here is where you will introduce yourself. What do you want to tell City Year about yourself and your background? Use this space to write notes.

_____

_____

_____

Paragraph 2

This is the most important part of the letter. Here is where you will talk about your specific interests in City Year's programs. Here is where you will ask them for something—a brochure, more information, or maybe a phone call from someone who can answer your questions. Use this space to write notes.

_____

_____

_____

_____

Paragraph 3

This is the conclusion of the letter. Here is where you restate your main point, thank the person receiving the letter, and close the letter. Use this space to write notes.

_____

_____

_____

Name _____ Date _____

● Writing Assignment
Use with student book page 315.
Writing Support

> **Grammar: Irregular Verbs**
> An irregular verb forms its past tense in a different way than a regular verb.
> Sometimes, the spelling of the verb changes. Other times, the verb does not change
> at all in the past tense.
>
> | Infinitive | Past Tense | Infinitive | Past Tense |
> |---|---|---|---|
> | write | wrote | swim | swam |
> | catch | caught | bite | bit |
> | know | knew | sit | sat |
> | set | set | speak | spoke |

A. Fix the errors with past tense verbs in the following sentences.

swam
Example: We ~~swum~~ in the lake at summer camp.

1. I knowed all of the answers on the social studies test.

2. A City Year leader spoken to our school at an assembly last week.

3. I writed a letter to City Year asking for more information.

4. Ignacio's dog bite his friend yesterday.

5. Manuel hit the baseball into left field, but the other team catched the ball.

6. We all set down when the teacher came into the classroom.

7. Helen cooked dinner while I setted the table.

B. Use three irregular past tense verbs to talk about things you did to help others.

Example: *I went to a homeless shelter and gave out sandwiches.*

1. _____

2. _____

3. _____

● **Writing Assignment**
Revising Activity

Use with student book page 315.

Read the business letter.

12B Vista Street
Quincy, MA 02171

Margaret Wright
English Action
2222 Main Street
Somerville, MA 02143

(1) Dear Margaret:

(2) I am very interested in your program. Could you send me more information? I'm Ignacio, and I'm from Colombia. I've lived in the U.S. for six months, but my English is very good.

(3) Sincerely,
    Ignacio

Identify the problems with the following parts of the letter.

1. In the salutation (1), the writer should
   a. use a comma instead of a colon.
   b. address the person as **Ms. Wright** instead of **Margaret.**
   c. use the word **dearest** instead of **dear.**
   d. use a complete sentence.

2. One problem with the body (2) is that
   a. the writer should introduce himself first.
   b. the writer should be specific about which program interests him.
   c. the writer should not use such informal language.
   d. all of the above.

3. The problem with the closing (3) is
   a. the writer doesn't give his full name.
   b. the writer should use a colon instead of a comma.
   c. the word **sincerely** is too informal.
   d. all of the above.

4. One thing missing from the letter is
   a. the date.
   b. a concluding paragraph.
   c. a signature.
   d. all of the above.

Name _____ Date _____

● Writing Assignment
Editing Activity

Use with student book page 315.

Read this brief business letter and fix the errors in spelling, capitalization, punctuation, and word usage. Mark the mistakes using the editing marks on page 455 of your student book.

Dear Mr Golding

My name is Samuel Cruz. I speaked to you a few days ago on the fone, but I thought I should follow up with a letter. By next June, I will completed the sixth grade, and I would like to volunteer in the summer. I had heard a lot about your language-exchange program with American kids, and it sounds interesting. I am from the Filippines, and I speak Tagalog and spanish. I should emfasize that my grammar and spelling are perphect. So, I have a lot to offer! I would appreciate it if you could send me the following items

a brochure
an application
materials to prepare for the program

Thank you very much for your help!
Sincerely Samuel Cruz

Now rewrite the letter. Make the changes you marked above.

_____

_____

_____

_____

_____

_____

_____

_____

_____

Name _____ Date _____

● Vocabulary From the Reading

Use with student book page 320.

> **Key Vocabulary**
>
> device   incident
> fine-tune   launch
> garbled   motivate

A. Write the Key Vocabulary word for each definition. Then unscramble the circled letters to spell a new word meaning "something new and useful."

Example: to make perfect: <u>f</u> <u>i</u> <u>n</u> <u>e</u> - <u>t</u> <u>u</u>(<u>n</u>)<u>e</u>

1. to push; to inspire: _◯_◯_ _◯_

2. useful object or piece of equipment: _ _◯◯_ _

3. to send off; to release; to put into motion: _ _ _◯_ _

4. to distort; to mix up sounds: _ _ _ _ _◯_

5. event; something that happened: _◯_ _ _ _◯_

6. something new and useful: ◯◯◯◯◯◯◯◯◯

B. Complete each sentence with the correct form of a Key Vocabulary word.

Example: The company _____launched_____ its new product yesterday.

1. I didn't understand you on the telephone. You sounded _____.

2. I wrote a rough draft of my composition, but I need to _____ it before I give it to the teacher.

3. My father bought a new _____ for the kitchen that automatically mixes and bakes bread.

4. Victor would like to forget the embarrassing _____ at the restaurant last year.

5. NASA is going to _____ another space ship to the moon.

6. The teacher will _____ her students by offering prizes for the best essays.

Name _____ Date _____

● Reading Strategy

Use with student book page 321.

Analyze Text Structure

Text structure is the way an author organizes his or her ideas in a text. Some examples of **logical** text structure, which you have already learned, are cause/effect, compare/contrast, and description.

Academic Vocabulary for the Reading Strategy	
Word	**Explanation**
structure	the way that parts are put together or organized
propose	to suggest or recommend
logical	showing good sense or reason

Read the paragraphs written by a student for the school paper.

1. We use too much electricity in our school. This is not only a waste of money for the school, but it is also bad for the environment. There are many things that students, teachers, and administrators can do right now to help.

2. First, we should all turn off lights in classrooms and bathrooms that we are not using. Next, we should use long-lasting, energy-efficient lightbulbs in all rooms and energy-efficient appliances in the cafeteria and teachers' lounge. Finally, we should unplug any equipment that we are not using.

3. If we can save on electric bills, maybe we can use that money toward much-needed supplies and school programs, like art, theater, and sports. Also, anything we can do to help the environment will help us all in the long run.

Now, complete the flowchart with information from the reading.

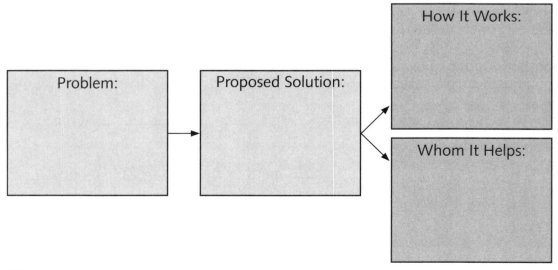

Name _____ Date _____

● Text Genre

Use with student book page 322.

Informational Text: Magazine Article

Magazine Article	
organization	order, or structure, of the material presented in the article
coherence	clarity of order; having every sentence, paragraph, and section in an order that helps a reader to understand the subject
unity	the sense that all of the material in an article is related or connected in some way

Read the excerpt from an article.

Saving Electricity at Home

You may not be able to afford solar panels or a wind generator right now. However, you can save money—and the environment—with just a few adjustments to your home and your lifestyle. Obviously, you should turn off any appliance or light you are not using.

Money spent now may be money saved later

Energy-saving lightbulbs are more expensive at the store, but they last longer and use less electricity than other bulbs, so in the long run they save money. If you are buying new appliances, look for the energy efficiency rating on the label. Again, an efficient appliance might have a higher price tag, but you will pay less later on your electric bills. Did you know that appliances and chargers that are left plugged in actually continue to draw electricity even when the appliance is not on or the charger is not charging? This could be costing you extra!

Some basic actions you can take today to save electricity

Here are some tips on how you can become more energy efficient at home...

Answer the following questions:

1. The first paragraph has problems with organization and coherence. Which sentence doesn't belong? Where should it be moved to?

   _____

2. There is information in the second paragraph that doesn't belong there. What is it?

   _____

3. Are there any problems with unity in the article? Is there any information that doesn't belong in the article?

   _____

Name _____ Date _____

● Reading Comprehension

Use with student book page 329.

Academic Vocabulary for the Reading Comprehension Questions	
promote	to support; to contribute to the progress or growth of
outcome	end result or effect

A. **Summarize the article.** Briefly explain each invention described in the article.

_____

_____

_____

_____

_____

B. **Write your response.** What kind of invention would you like to create for your home, school, or community? Why? How would you promote it?

_____

_____

_____

_____

_____

C. **Assess the reading strategy.** You have practiced identifying problems and their solutions. What was the outcome of using this strategy?

_____

_____

_____

_____

_____

Name _____ Date _____

● Text Element
Definitions

Use with student book page 329.

Many magazine articles offer new information to readers. To help readers understand this material, articles often include definitions, or explanations, of words and phrases. In this way, an article can teach vocabulary that is specific to the article's topic.

Read the passage and find three words or phrases that are defined in it.

A blender is a very popular electrical appliance, or device, that can be found in almost every kitchen. It is used for chopping, liquefying, pureeing, and mixing ingredients. The modern blender has sharp rotating blades at the bottom of a tall plastic or glass container. A Polish inventor named Stephen Poplawski was the first to patent—that is, to obtain legal recognition for inventing—the blender in 1922. This early blender was used primarily at soda fountains, which were shops or shop counters where people could sit and order milk shakes. Other inventors came along and improved on the blender design over the years, including Fred Waring and John Oster. You can see their names on blenders today.

Write three words or phrases from the passage above. Then write the definitions.

Example: _appliance_

Meaning: _device_

1. Word: _____

   Meaning: _____

2. Word: _____

   Meaning: _____

3. Word: _____

   Meaning: _____

Name _____   Date _____

● Vocabulary From the Reading

Use with student book page 330.

> **Key Vocabulary**
>
> abolish   sacrifice
> generosity   summon
> mortal

A.   Replace the underlined phrase with a Key Vocabulary word.

Example: We really appreciate your <u>giving nature</u>. *generosity* _____

1.   The principal <u>called</u> all the students to the auditorium. _____

2.   We are all <u>earthly</u> beings; we will not live forever. _____

3.   My parents <u>gave up</u> a lot in order to come to this country. _____

4.   In what year did the United States <u>get rid of</u> slavery? _____

5.   Thanks to the townspeople's <u>kindness</u>, the stranger had a warm meal and a

place to stay for the night. _____

B.   Answer each question with complete sentences.

1.   What sacrifice have you made? _____

_____

2.   Can you think of a practice, other than slavery, that has been abolished in this

country or in your home country? When? _____

_____

3.   When have you demonstrated generosity? What did you do? _____

_____

4.   Have you ever been summoned to someone's office or to a meeting? Who? Why?

_____

_____

Name _____ Date _____

● Reading Strategy
Recognize Author's Style

Use with student book page 331.

> **Recognizing an author's writing style** is like thinking about someone's personality. Some authors use big words; others use shorter words. Some people have strong personalities; some authors write with strong ideas and vivid words. Some authors like to use images and description, while other authors focus on action.

To recognize the characteristics of an author's style, ask yourself these questions as you read the passage below:

1. Does the author choose big or small words? Does he or she use formal or informal language?

   _____

2. Does the author write in long or short sentences? Does he or she repeat ideas?

   _____

3. Are the author's ideas simple, or are they complicated?

   _____

4. Does the author directly address the audience? Who is the audience?

   _____

Friends, fellow students: I just want to talk to you a little bit about improving our school community. We're all good people. We're all smart people. But we don't always show the best part of ourselves, do we? Sometimes I see a kid eating lunch alone in the cafeteria. Sometimes I see a kid whose books have fallen on the floor, and no one is helping him. Sometimes—sometimes—I even see kids being mean to other kids. Come on, everyone! We're better than that! I want to ask each one of you to close your eyes and remember a time when you felt alone, when you had a problem. When you were in a new place and didn't know anyone. How would you want someone else to act toward you in that situation? To ignore you? To walk by? To laugh at you? Let me ask you all this, now: When do you feel better about yourselves—when you help people or when you ignore them? When you smile at someone or when you frown? When you relieve someone's pain or when you cause it? I want you all to think about this. Really **think** about it. Let's start showing our best side, everyone!

Name _____ Date _____

● Text Genre
Use with student book page 331.
Speech

Speech	
audience	the listeners to a speech; a speech often addresses the audience directly.
vivid language	strong, descriptive, active words or imagery
repetition	using a word or phrase two or more times to make a point or create a sense of rhythm

A. Read this excerpt from a speech by Susan B. Anthony, who fought for women's right to vote. She gave this speech in 1873 after she was arrested for voting in an election. Circle at least two examples of vivid language.

1. Friends and fellow citizens: I stand before you tonight under **indictment**[1] for the **alleged**[2] crime of having voted at the last presidential election... The **preamble**[3] of the Federal Constitution says: "We, the people of the United States, in order to form a more perfect union, establish justice... and secure the **blessings**[4] of liberty to ourselves and our **posterity**[5], do ordain and establish this Constitution for the United States of America."

2. It was we, the people; not we, the white male citizens; nor yet we, the male citizens; but we, the whole people, who formed the Union. And we formed it, not to give the blessings of liberty, but to secure them; not to the half of ourselves and the half of our posterity, but to the whole people—women as well as men.

B. Answer the questions.

1. Which sentence or phrase shows you that Susan B. Anthony is directly addressing an audience? Who do you think her audience might be?

_____

2. Describe two examples of Susan B. Anthony's use of repetition in her speech.

_____

_____

_____

---

[1] **indictment:** formal accusation in court
[2] **alleged:** something that is claimed
[3] **preamble:** beginning

[4] **blessings:** benefits, things that bring happiness
[5] **posterity:** those who come after us

Name _____ Date _____

● Reading Comprehension

Use with student book page 335.

A. **Summarize the speech.** In your own words, explain what Kennedy was trying to tell the people in his speech.

_____

_____

_____

_____

_____

B. **Write your response.** What are some ways that a person can serve his or her country? What would you be willing to do for your country?

_____

_____

_____

_____

_____

C. **Assess the reading strategy.** As you read Kennedy's speech, you were asked to look for the author's style. Did this help you understand the speech better? How?

_____

_____

_____

_____

Name _____ Date _____

● **Spelling**
Commonly Misspelled Words

Use with student book page 335.

Review this list of words from the two readings.

building: structure; house	**solemn:** serious; somber
circuit: an electrical connection	**success:** victory; triumph
committed: dedicated; loyal	**truly:** in a true way; really
conscience: a sense of right and wrong	**tyranny:** oppressive rule; dictatorship
heir: one who inherits something	**wrist:** joint that connects the hand to the arm

A. Circle the ten words in the grid. They can appear horizontally, diagonally, or vertically. One of the words appears backward.

U	C	A	B	U	I	L	D	I	N	G	S	Y	Y	E	C	E	E	W	S	C
S	E	I	C	U	G	E	U	R	M	Y	O	G	W	I	C	N	L	Y	R	D
I	S	Y	R	T	I	L	O	R	E	N	L	N	R	T	L	D	C	R	I	S
I	N	N	O	C	S	S	T	Y	R	I	E	R	T	C	Y	M	R	C	R	T
U	T	R	C	C	U	I	N	O	R	M	M	E	M	N	L	R	U	S	U	R
I	H	L	E	G	C	I	D	I	S	I	N	E	S	E	S	I	A	I	S	U
T	S	E	C	I	O	I	T	S	R	W	C	C	E	S	I	I	D	N	I	E
S	R	T	I	T	C	W	T	R	U	L	Y	C	E	T	T	E	S	U	N	L
M	I	C	S	R	C	N	R	Y	T	D	E	C	L	L	T	G	I	E	U	Y
S	I	I	R	C	I	U	S	R	G	E	C	C	N	T	U	I	C	R	I	C
S	S	S	W	C	E	U	Y	R	G	U	L	N	I	L	R	R	I	I	L	Y
I	W	R	I	S	T	N	E	S	S	I	S	M	S	U	C	I	T	N	N	U
R	N	N	T	N	A	C	G	R	N	T	M	R	T	C	R	E	I	N	I	H
D	I	D	S	R	E	T	R	T	Y	O	M	S	O	N	E	H	I	O	M	Y
I	U	S	Y	S	E	I	G	S	C	E	C	N	E	I	C	S	N	O	C	C
E	N	C	O	N	C	I	E	N	S	E	T	S	S	B	O	C	T	S	C	E

B. Correct the spelling in the following sentences.

                  i   ui   ui
Example: The electrical curciuts in the bilding need to be repaired.

2. The good prince was the hair to the throne, but his father's rule was one of tyrany and oppression.

3. The party on Saturday was truely a sucess.

4. I hurt my rist playing tennis.

5. We are solemly comitted to serving our country.

218

Name _____ Date _____

● Writing Conventions
Use with student book page 335.

Punctuation: Using Ellipses and Brackets

> **Ellipses**
>
> Use ellipses (...) to show where text is removed from an excerpt:
> *"Let every nation know, whether it wishes us well or ill, that we shall pay any price...*
> *to assure the survival and the success of liberty...." —John F. Kennedy*

A. Remove some text from the following quotes to make them shorter without changing their basic meaning. Use ellipses to show where you removed text.

Example: It was we, the people; not we, the white male citizens; nor yet we, the male citizens; but we, the whole people, who formed the Union.

It was we, the people...we, the whole people, who formed the Union.

1. In your hands, my fellow citizens, more than mine, will rest the final success or failure of our course.

_____

2. We observe today not a victory of party, but a celebration of freedom—symbolizing an end, as well as a beginning—signifying renewal, as well as change.

_____

_____

> **Brackets**
>
> Use brackets to fill in needed words in a quote:
> *"[The project] took science out of the classroom," says Joyce, "and put it in real life."*

B. Add the missing information into the quotes. Use brackets.

Example: "It works almost like a walkie-talkie," she says. (from an article about the IllumaCoach)

"[The IllumaCoach] works almost like a walkie-talkie," she says.

1. "The Navajo soldiers had to get it right every time." (referring to Navajo code)

_____

2. "His writings are both revered and controversial," explained the professor. (talking about Benito Juárez)

_____

Name _____ Date _____

● Vocabulary Development

Use with student book page 337.

Word Order

Often in formal speech or writing, the speaker or writer changes the **order of the words** in a sentence to emphasize the meaning of certain phrases, or to make a word or idea more powerful. See the following example from "Inaugural Address:"

Original Sentence	Normal Word Order
"We observe today not a victory of party, but a celebration of freedom."	"Today we are observing a celebration of freedom, not a party's victory."

A. What do you think would be the normal word order for the following sentences, following the example above?

Original Sentence	Normal Word Order
1. "In your hands, my fellow citizens, more than mine, will rest the final success or failure of our course."	_____ _____ _____ _____ _____
2. "...[A]sk not what your country can do for you; ask what you can do for your country."	_____ _____ _____ _____
3. "[A]sk not what America will do for you, but what together we can do for the freedom of man."	_____ _____ _____ _____ _____
4. "With a good conscience our only sure reward, with history the final judge of our deeds, let us go forth to lead the land we love..."	_____ _____ _____ _____

B. Go back to the chart in Exercise A. Underline the words that are emphasized or made more powerful in the original sentences from the speech.

Name _____ Date _____

● Grammar

Use with student book pages 338–339.

Verbals: Infinitives, Gerunds, and Participles

A **verbal** is a word that comes from a **verb** and expresses action or a state of being.

An **infinitive** is a verbal that functions as a noun or adverb. Form an infinitive by using the word **to** before a verb.

Infinitives		
example	part of speech	function
To dance onstage is exciting.	noun	subject of the sentence
She wanted **to play**.	noun	object of the verb *wanted*
The students study **to learn**.	adverb	modifies the verb *study*

A **gerund** is a verbal that functions as a noun. Form a gerund by adding **-ing** to a verb.

Gerunds		
example	part of speech	function
Dancing onstage is exciting.	noun	subject of the sentence
She wanted **acting** to be her career.	noun	object of the verb *wanted*
He will get in trouble for **driving** without a license.	noun	object of the preposition *for*

A **participle** is a verbal that is used as an adjective. It often ends in **-ing** or **-ed**. There are two kinds of participles: **present participles** and **past participles**. Form a present participle by adding **-ing** to a verb. Form a past participle by adding **-ed** to a verb.

Present Participles		
example	part of speech	function
The **chirping** birds woke me up.	adjective	modifies *birds*
The girl **playing** in the sand is my sister.	adjective	modifies *girl*

Past Participles		
example	part of speech	function
The book **published** ten years ago is still popular.	adjective	modifies *book*

Name _____ Date _____

A. Circle the verbal in each sentence. Label it as an infinitive, gerund, present participle, or past participle.

Example: _____infinitive_____ I need money (to buy) lunch in the cafeteria.

1. _____ Valerie spread some melted cheese on her bread.

2. _____ We love watching the Winter Olympics on television.

3. _____ The boy sitting in the front row is my friend Terence.

4. _____ To be a good friend is very important.

5. _____ Shopping is never fun for Ari and me.

B. Complete each sentence with a logical verbal form of the verb in parentheses. Next to the sentence, write what kind of verbal you used.

Example: I prefer the house __painted__ (paint) yellow. ____past participle____

1. Yesterday Cheryl ate _____ (roast) lamb. _____

2. Ken went to the store _____ (buy) new clothes. _____

3. We need _____ (read) ten pages tonight. _____

4. Do you really have a _____ (talk) parrot? _____

5. The teacher handed back the _____ (correct) exams. _____

C. Write a sentence using the indicated verbal.

Example: Use the past participle of the verb **give** as an adjective.
          I wore the watch given to me by my grandfather.

1. Use the infinitive of **write** as the object of a verb.

   _____

2. Use the gerund of **dance** as the subject of a sentence.

   _____

3. Use the present participle of **dance** as an adjective.

   _____

4. Use the past participle of **finish** as an adjective.

   _____

● Grammar Expansion
Verbs Followed by an Infinitive, a Gerund, or Either

When you follow a verb with a verbal, use the correct form. Some verbs can only be followed by an infinitive, while others can only be followed by a gerund. Some can be followed by either.

Verbs Followed by an Infinitive	
refuse	I refuse to do your homework for you.
want	I wanted to go with you.
need	We need to study tonight.
decide	They decided to stay home today.
Verbs Followed by a Gerund	
keep	Keep walking; the store is at the end of this street.
stop	Stop talking so loudly!
practice	I practice speaking English with my friends.
enjoy	We really enjoy hiking and camping.
finish	Did you finish writing the essay?
Verbs Followed by a Gerund or an Infinitive	
continue	If you continue to study, you will continue getting good grades.
like	I like to read. I also like watching movies.
love	She loves to draw. She also loves painting.
start	I am starting to understand this. When will we start practicing it?
prefer	Would you prefer to dance or to sit? I prefer dancing to sitting.
try	Try to do these exercises. Try doing them quickly.

A. Circle the correct form of the verb.

Example: Did you enjoy ((listening) / to listen) to that CD?

1. I refuse (telling / to tell) the secret.

2. My brother finally stopped (snoring / to snore).

3. I do not want (to go / going) to the doctor.

4. She finished (making / to make) dinner.

5. I decided (eating / to eat) the apple.

6. You need to keep (practicing / to practice)!

Name _____ Date _____

B. Complete the sentences with the correct verbal form of the verb in the parentheses. Some items may have more than one correct answer.

Example: My dog loves ___swimming___ in the pond (swim).

1. We stopped _____ to that store when it was sold to a big chain. (go)

2. José likes to practice _____ his new guitar. (play)

3. You need to stop _____ about your pronunciation. It's fine! (worry)

4. You should try _____ along to songs in English. (sing)

5. Laura wants _____ Egypt someday. (visit)

6. If it starts _____, you should come back inside. (rain)

7. The boy's mother refused _____ him extra money. (give)

8. Vicki loves _____ at the beach, but she really prefers

    _____ scuba diving. (swim / go)

C. Complete the sentences with your own information. Use an infinitive or a gerund in each answer.

1. I enjoy _____.

2. My friends and I like _____.

3. My mother decided _____.

4. I want _____.

5. I started _____.

6. My friend refuses _____.

7. My teacher keeps _____.

8. I always try _____.

9. Our class continues _____.

10. Yesterday I finished _____.

Name _____ Date _____

● Writing Assignment
Response to Literature: Writing Style

Use with student book pages 340–341.

Use this chart to help you organize your thoughts before you write your essay.

1. Make a list of ways to describe Kennedy's writing style. Find an example in his writing for each description.

Description	Example
uses dramatic metaphors	"Now the trumpet summons us again..."

2. Now describe your own writing style. Consider how your style is different and in what ways it might be similar to Kennedy's.

_____

_____

_____

_____

_____

_____

_____

3. Now go back and number the descriptions of Kennedy's style from the most obvious point to the least obvious point. Do the same for the descriptions of your own style.

Name _____ Date _____

● Writing Assignment

Use with student book page 341.

Writing Support

> **Mechanics: Parallelism**
>
> Parallelism is the repetition of different ideas using the same grammatical structure. Parallelism can involve words, phrases, or whole sentences. Writers use parallelism to stress ideas or to create rhythm in their writing.
> - ...the truth, the whole truth, and nothing but the truth. (repeating words)
> - Give me liberty, or give me death! (repeating phrases)
> - Let freedom ring from the mighty mountains of New York.
>   Let freedom ring from the heightening Alleghenies of Pennsylvania.
>   Let freedom ring from the snowcapped Rockies of Colorado. (repeating sentences)

A. Underline the examples of parallelism in the following quotes.

Example: "It was <u>we, the people</u>; not <u>we, the white male citizens</u>; nor yet <u>we, the male citizens</u>; but <u>we, the whole people</u>, who formed the Union." —Susan B. Anthony

1. "I like to see a man proud of the place in which he lives. I like to see a man live so that his place will be proud of him." —Abraham Lincoln

2. What we need in the United States is not division; what we need in the United States is not hatred; what we need in the United States is not violence and lawlessness, but is love and wisdom, and compassion toward one another, and a feeling of justice toward those who still suffer within our country, whether they be white or whether they be black. —Robert F. Kennedy

3. I think we consider too much the good luck of the early bird and not enough the bad luck of the early worm. —Franklin D. Roosevelt

B. Find two examples of parallelism in Kennedy's "Inaugural Address."

1. _____

   _____

2. _____

   _____

C. Imagine you are giving a speech to your classmates on something you feel strongly about. Write two sentences delivering your message. Use parallelism.

1. _____

2. _____

Name _____ Date _____

● Writing Assignment
Revising Activity

Use with student book page 341.

Read your essay carefully. Answer the following questions. You may wish to use the answers to revise your essay.

1. Do you give an example for each description of Kennedy's writing? Does each example support and illustrate your point?

   _____

   _____

2. Do you give examples of your own writing style? Do your examples illustrate your descriptions of your own writing?

   _____

3. Do you have an introductory paragraph to open your essay? Does it include a thesis statement? After writing the whole essay, does the thesis statement still fit the essay, or do you need to revise it? Use this space for notes.

   _____

   _____

4. In the body of your essay, do you compare or contrast Kennedy's style to your own? Your paragraph about Kennedy and your paragraph about yourself should have parallel structures. This gives your essay unity. Reread the second two paragraphs in the student model, then reread your own paragraphs. Do you need to make any changes?

   _____

   _____

   _____

5. Do you have a concluding paragraph that summarizes and restates your main idea? This paragraph should not contain any new information. Do you need to add or revise this paragraph? Use this space for notes.

   _____

   _____

   _____

Name _____ Date _____

● Writing Assignment

Use with student book page 341.

Editing Activity

A. Read this paragraph and fix the errors in spelling, punctuation, capitalization, and word usage. Mark the mistakes using the editing marks on page 455 of your student book.

Friends, classmates, fellow students. I stand before you on this solem occasion—the day before final exams—not to scare you, not to worry you, not bore you, but to wish you all good luck and sucess. To taking an exam is a difficult and important task, a task that requires a clear concience and a heart that is truely commited and wants doing its best. as Principal Linsky observed in his speech on opening day, "Kennedy Junior High] is now the number one school in the state..... be proud of your school, and make your school proud of you"

B. Now rewrite the paragraph. Make the changes you marked above.

_____

_____

_____

_____

_____

_____

_____

_____

_____

_____

_____

_____

_____

_____

Name _____ Date _____

● Vocabulary From the Reading

Use with student book page 358.

> **Key Vocabulary**
>
> companion   immense
> courageous   timid
> distribute   tireless

A. Write the Key Vocabulary word for each definition.

Example: ____tireless____ determined; diligent; showing no signs of weariness or exhaustion

Word	Definition
1. _____	to hand out; to give
2. _____	shy
3. _____	a friend; person or animal that one spends time with
4. _____	very large
5. _____	brave

B. In each sentence, fill in the blank with a Key Vocabulary word. Make sure to use the correct form of the word.

Example: The teacher will ____distribute____ the exam papers.

1. It was very _____ to save the little girl's dog.

2. Lorena is very _____; she doesn't talk very much in class.

3. The plate of noodles was _____; I couldn't finish it!

4. Our _____ efforts at the science fair paid off; we won first place!

5. The man and his _____ sat down at the restaurant table.

C. Write two sentences using the Key Vocabulary words.

Example: _I went to a Chinese restaurant with my soccer companions after the game._

1. _____

2. _____

Name _____ Date _____

● Reading Strategy

Use with student book page 359.

Analyze Character

> To **analyze a character,** look for details that reveal the personality of a person in a story. Think about descriptions of the character and the **dialogues** that **justify** his or her interaction with other characters. Also consider what characters have to say about each other.

Academic Vocabulary for the Reading Strategy	
Word	**Explanation**
dialogue	a conversation between two or more people or characters
justify	to give a reason for an action

As you read the passage, look for details about the main character's personality. Write your first impression of the character in the first box. Then fill in details about the character. Is your final character analysis consistent with your first impression?

1 Patty strolled into class fifteen minutes late. She coughed loudly, then slowly took her seat in the front row. Ms. Ochoa put down the piece of chalk she had been using to write grammar charts on the board, and marched over to Patty's desk. "Miss O'Connor!" she barked. "Class begins at 8:10. Do you know what time it is?"

2 "Sure, ma'am," Patty answered. "It's 8:25 and 30 seconds."

3 "I want to see you here after school at 2:18 and 0 seconds. Do you hear me?"

4 "Of course I hear you," Patty answered. "You're yelling in my ear."

5 The other students looked stunned. Some students gasped. Some exchanged looks of disbelief. But no one dared to laugh or say anything.

First Impression of _____:

| How the Character Is Described: | What He or She Tells Us: | What Others Tell Us About Him or Her: |

Final Character Analysis:

Name _____ Date _____

● Text Genre
Novel

Use with student book page 360.

Novel	
characters	the people in a novel or story
mood	the feeling the author wants the reader to get while reading scenes or moments in the novel
setting	where and when a story takes place
conflict	a problem or struggle at the center of a story

A. Read the passages and identify the setting, mood, characters, and conflict of each one.

Example: I woke up sweating. I looked at my alarm clock. I still had three hours before I needed to get up for school.

1. The setting: _a student's bedroom_____

2. The mood: _____

3. The characters: _____

4. The conflict: _____

B. "What do you want?" growled the impatient young woman with dark circles under her eyes. I smiled weakly and said, "I'll have the cheese omelette, please."

1. The setting: _____

2. The mood: _____

3. The characters: _____ and _____

4. The conflict: _____

C. It was a beautiful book filled with fantastic illustrations bound in a red leather cover with gold lettering. Mrs. Evans saw the price tag and shook her head. "Please?" I asked.

1. The setting: _____

2. The mood: _____

3. The characters: _____ and _____

4. The conflict: _____

Name _____ Date _____

● Reading Comprehension

Use with student book page 371.

Academic Vocabulary for the Reading Comprehension Questions	
Word	Explanation
affect	to influence or have an impact on someone or something
judge	to consider something and then give an official decision

A. **Retell the story.** Retell *Iqbal* in your own words.

_____

_____

_____

_____

_____

_____

_____

B. **Write your response.** Iqbal told Eshan Khan that he was not afraid of anybody. Based on evidence in the story, judge whether this statement is true.

_____

_____

_____

_____

C. **Assess the reading strategy.** How did analyzing Iqbal's character affect your understanding of the story?

_____

_____

_____

_____

Name _____   Date _____

● Literary Element
Simile

Use with student book page 371.

> A **simile** is a comparison of two different or unlikely things. Similes use the words **like** or **as** to make these comparisons. Even though a simile compares things that seem very different, a simile highlights the shared characteristics of these two things.

A. Complete the similes.

Example: __*a*__ Mr. Taylor's suit looked just like

1. _____ The room was as hot as	**a.** ~~a couch cover.~~
2. _____ The bread we left on the table was as hard as	**b.** a bulldog.
3. _____ Her hand was cold like	**c.** a block of ice.
4. _____ The gym teacher, Mr. Connelly, is as mean as	**d.** a rock.
5. _____ In her new beautiful dress, Priscilla looked like	**e.** an oven.
6. _____ The chewy, flavorless pizza crust was like	**f.** cardboard.
	g. a queen.

B. Complete the following similes with an appropriate word.

Example: The bride's dress was as white as _____snow_____.

1. The teacher was so angry, her face became as red as _____.

2. My backpack is so heavy, it feels like _____ on my back.

3. The air-conditioning was so strong, it felt like _____.

4. Beni runs as fast as _____. He always wins races!

C. Write your own similes to describe the following items.

1. What you had for lunch yesterday

_____

2. An item of clothing you love

_____

3. A person you know

_____

Name _____ Date _____

● Vocabulary From the Reading

Use with student book page 372.

> **Key Vocabulary**
>
> | | |
> |---|---|
> | activist | contribution |
> | advocate | negotiate |
> | boycott | reform |

A. Choose the correct definition for each Key Vocabulary word.

Example: __b__ negotiate: a. to refuse to buy b. to make a deal c. to fight for	2. _____ boycott: a. justice b. refusal to buy something c. a protest march	4. _____ reform: a. change; correction b. protest; revolt c. injustice; harm
1. _____ advocate: a. to call a meeting b. to march in protest c. to support; to fight for	3. _____ activist: a. an athlete b. someone who fights for a cause c. a migrant worker	5. _____ contribution: a. activity b. a speech c. something given

B. Complete each sentence with a Key Vocabulary word. Be sure to use the correct form of the word.

Example: The _____ *boycott* _____ helped them improve working conditions.

1. Iqbal was a young Pakistani _____.

2. Iqbal _____ for the liberation of child workers.

3. My mother made a _____ of $100 to Save the Children.

4. The citizens called for a _____ of the country's strict laws.

C. Answer the questions using the Key Vocabulary words. Tell the truth.

1. Are there any school policies or systems that you think need reform? Why?

_____

2. Would you ever boycott something? Why?

_____

3. Describe something you have had to negotiate.

_____

234

Name _____ Date _____

● Reading Strategy
Identify the Main Idea

Use with student book page 373.

> **Identifying the main idea** of a piece of writing helps you understand the central message. In informational texts, the main idea is surrounded by facts and details. As a reader, you must identify the main idea in order to better understand how the details relate to it.

Write the main idea of each paragraph.

At the age of four, Iqbal Masih was forced into bonded labor by his parents. He was supposed to be freed when his family's loan was paid, but years passed and he continued to work under miserable conditions in a carpet factory. At the age of ten, Iqbal escaped and joined a human rights organization that helped other children in the same situation. He spoke publicly against the practice of forced child labor. Because of his young age and extraordinary courage, Iqbal is a great source of inspiration for activists and ordinary people alike.

1. **Main idea:** _____

   _____

Francesco D'Adamo has written books for all ages, but he specializes in issues affecting children and young adults. He has won awards for his children's books. *Iqbal* is the first of D'Adamo's books to be published in the U.S. Another of his books that has been translated into English is *My Brother Johnny,* a novel about war and its consequences.

2. **Main idea:** _____

   _____

The island of Puerto Rico is a mix of many different cultures. The Taínos, an indigenous tribe, lived there when Columbus landed on the island in 1493. Puerto Rico belonged to Spain for more than four centuries, so Spanish is spoken there, and Puerto Rican culture has strong Spanish roots. A notable African influence is also present, especially in music, art, and many traditions. Today, Puerto Rico is a commonwealth of the United States, and Puerto Ricans are U.S. citizens. As a result, American culture has a strong presence on the island and many people speak English or use English words.

3. **Main idea:** _____

   _____

Name _____ Date _____

● Text Genre

Use with student book page 373.

Informational Text: Social Studies Textbook

Social Studies Textbooks	
primary sources	documents created at the time of an event or quotation from a person who lived at that time
summaries	brief statements that cover the most important features of a reading selection
boxed items	comments or activities that relate to but are separate from the main text; they often appear to the side of the main reading

Read the sentences. Write **T** for **true** and **F** for **false.**

1. _____ You are reading about Martin Luther King, Jr. in a textbook. An example of a primary source would be an excerpt of a biography of King.

2. _____ Another example of a primary source would be a letter written by King.

3. _____ You are writing a report about Iqbal. A good primary source would be Francesco D'Adamo's novel.

4. _____ Another source might be a transcript of Iqbal's Reebok-Youth-in-Action Award Acceptance Speech.

5. _____ A summary includes the main idea of a reading selection.

6. _____ A boxed item could contain vocabulary words from a reading selection.

7. _____ A boxed item could be a photo.

8. _____ A summary in a textbook is an example of a primary source.

9. _____ Boxed items usually appear in the back of a textbook.

10. _____ A summary could appear as a boxed item.

Name _____ Date _____

● Reading Comprehension

Use with student book page 379.

A. Retell the story. Summarize the main ideas of "The Equal Rights Struggle Expands."

_____

_____

_____

_____

_____

_____

B. Write your response. Why do you think it was important for the farm workers to engage in a nonviolent fight?

_____

_____

_____

_____

_____

C. Assess the reading strategy. How did finding the main idea of each section help you understand the story?

_____

_____

_____

_____

_____

Name _____ Date _____

● Spelling

Use with student book page 379.

The Suffixes -er and -or

The suffixes **-er** and **-or** can be added to many verbs to form nouns. The noun refers to a person or thing that performs the action of a verb.

Verb	Noun
labor	labor**er** (a person who labors)
lend money	moneylend**er** (a person who lends money)
liberate	libera**tor** (a person who liberates)
refrigerate	refrigera**tor** (a machine that refrigerates)

Spelling rule: If the verb ends in a silent **e**, drop it before adding a suffix.

A. Replace the underlined phrase with a noun ending in the suffix **-er.**

Example: The person who owned the farm was unjust. ____*owner*____

1. The person who spoke was very persuasive. _____

2. Our person who employs us treats us well. _____

3. Every person who votes should know his or her rights. _____

B. Replace the underlined phrase with a noun ending in the suffix **-or.**

1. The president has many people who advise him. _____

2. Iqbal should have had more people to protect him. _____

3. They are the people who oppressed them. _____

C. Write a definition for each of the underlined words.

Example: Iqbal fought against exploiters of children.

  people who exploit other people _____

1. The conductor gave the signal for the violins to start playing.

  _____

2. The farm workers united in protest.

  _____

3. The grape growers were mistreating them.

  _____

Name _____   Date _____

● Writing Conventions
Spelling: Contractions

Use with student book page 379.

We often use contractions of auxiliary verb forms in informal speech and writing.

Present (Negative) of *be*	
I am not → I'm not	we are not → we're not / we aren't
he is not → he's not / he isn't	you are not → you're not / you aren't
she is not → she's not / she isn't	they are not → they're not / they aren't
it is not → it's not / it isn't	**Note:** There is no contraction with **am not.**

Negative of *do*	Negative of *did*	Past Negative of *be*	Negative of *have*
do not → don't	did not → didn't	was not → wasn't	has not → hasn't
does not → doesn't		were not → weren't	have not → haven't

Simple Present of *have*		would and had	
I have → I've	we have → we've	I'd	we'd
he has → he's	you have → you've	he'd	you'd
she has → she's	they have → they've	she'd	they'd
it has → it's		**It'd** (not common)	

Negative of *had*	Negative of *would*	Negative of *will*
had not → hadn't	would not → wouldn't	will not → won't

A. Rewrite the sentences using contractions.

Example: She does not like onions.   *She doesn't like onions.*

1. I have been to Peru, but she has not.   _____

2. I will not go if you do not want me to.   _____

3. They are not ready for the test.   _____

4. We had already eaten, but they had not.   _____

5. He did not say if he would come today.   _____

B. Write three true sentences about you and your family. Use contractions.

1. _____

2. _____

3. _____

Name _____ Date _____

● Vocabulary Development
Suffix: -ion

Use with student book page 381.

> The suffix **-ion** changes a word into a noun. For example, the verb **impress** changes to a noun when it becomes **impression. Isolate** becomes the noun **isolation**. Note that spelling changes are sometimes necessary.

A. Remove the suffix to transform each noun into a verb.

Example: confusion _____*confuse*_____

1. calculation _____

2. confession _____

3. fusion _____

4. perforation _____

5. digression _____

B. Add a suffix to the verbs in the box. Then complete the sentences with the correct noun.

Add a -tion ending:			Add an -sion ending:		
~~ignite~~	liberate	illustrate	explode	conclude	discuss

Example: A little spark caused the _____*ignition*_____ of the gasoline tank.

1. I really enjoyed the movie up until the _____, which I hated.

2. In class, we had a _____ about the book we read.

3. Iqbal fought for the _____ of child laborers.

4. They heard a loud _____ outside the building. Someone was sending a warning to Iqbal!

5. My social studies report had an _____ of a Mayan pyramid.

Name _____ Date _____

● Grammar
Conditional Clauses

Use with student book pages 382–383.

Use condition clauses beginning with **if, unless,** and **even if** to express:

- A real or possible situation that occurs in the present. Both the condition clause and the main clause will be in the present tense.

  If you heat the ice, it melts.

  You make mistakes **even if you try to be careful.**

- A real or possible situation in the future. The condition clause will be in the present tense, and the main clause will be in the future tense.

  If you let go of the rope, the flag will come down.

  Your feet will get wet **if you walk through the puddle.**

  Unless you do your homework, you will not get a good grade on the test.

A. Choose the correct verbs to complete the sentences.

Example: I won't eat the pizza if it ((has)/ will have) pepperoni on it.

1. If you (eat / will eat) too much food, you will get a stomachache.

2. I never drink orange juice unless it (is / will be) freshly squeezed.

3. Even if it rains tonight, we (go / will go) to the outdoor concert.

4. Unless you (tell / will tell) me your secret, I (don't / won't) tell you my secret.

5. I (finish / will finish) my book report even if it (takes / will take) all day.

B. Complete the sentences with your own ideas.

Example: Even if I lose the game, _I will congratulate the other team._

1. You will do well in school if _____.

2. If you learn English, _____.

3. I always go to school unless _____.

4. Even if it costs a lot of money, _____.

5. If my friend calls me tonight, _____.

6. Unless I feel too tired, _____.

Name _____ Date _____

Condition clauses can also be used to express unreal or imaginary situations. See the examples below.

- An unreal situation in the present describes what would happen in an imaginary situation:

  If I had more time, I would read more.

  We would go to the party **if Dad gave us permission.**

  If Matthew walked a little faster, the group would arrive on time.

To create these sentences, use the following structure:

Condition clause (**If** + past tense), main clause (**would** + verb)

Main clause (**would** + verb) . . . condition clause (**if** + past tense)

Note: When using the verb **to be** in the condition clause, use **were** instead of **was** for subjects **I, he, she,** and **it.**

  If I were older, I would have a driver's license.

  If she were the captain of the team, she would choose different uniforms.

- An unreal situation in the past describes how something could have happened differently:

  If I had gone to the game, I would have caught that fly ball.

  He would have gone to the party **if he had been invited.**

To create these sentences, use the following structure:

Condition clause (**If** +), main clause (**would have** + past participle)

Main clause (**would have** + past participle) . . . condition clause (**if** + past perfect tense)

C. Match the sentence beginnings to their correct and logical endings.

Example: __b__ If you are hungry,   a. we wouldn't get good grades.

1. _____ If I had more time,   b. ~~we can eat at my house.~~

2. _____ He would have come to the party   c. we won't pass the exam.

3. _____ If we don't study,   d. if he knew about it.

4. _____ If we didn't study,   e. I'd stay and talk to you.

5. _____ He would be angry   f. if we had called him.

Name _____ Date _____

D. Fill in the blanks with the correct form of the verb in parentheses.

Example: If I had a dog, I _____*would take*_____ him to this park. (take)

1. If you _____ to my house, we would have studied together. (come)

2. If my parents _____ a car, they would travel more. (buy)

3. She would buy the DVD if she _____ enough money. (have)

4. He would have eaten lunch if I _____ it for him. (prepare)

5. I usually get the fish if they _____ it. (have)

6. Justin _____ a band if he could play an instrument. (join)

7. I would _____ my homework if I had time. (do)

8. If you didn't know the answer, you should _____. (ask)

E. Complete the sentences with your own ideas. Use the correct verb form.

Example: If I were older, __*I would travel the world*_____.

1. If I could drive a car, _____.

2. If I finish my homework early, _____.

3. I would have been very angry if _____.

4. I would be very happy if _____.

5. I would be sad if _____.

6. If we have time this weekend, _____.

7. If I had an airplane, _____.

8. I would help someone if _____.

Name _____   Date _____

● Grammar Expansion
Conditional Expressions with Modals: should, could, and might

You can use these modal verbs in present and future real situations:

Modal	Expresses	Example
should	advice	If it rains, you **should** take an umbrella.
could	a possibility or ability	If it rains, you **could** go to the movies or stay in.
might	a possibility	If it rains, we **might** still go out.

You can also use these modal expressions in unreal past situations:

Modal	Expresses	Example
should have	advice that was not taken or known	—He didn't wear a coat. It was cold. —He should have worn a coat if it was cold.
could have	a past possibility that did not happen	—I stayed home alone. I didn't call you. —If you had called me, we could have talked.
might have	a guess about what possibly happened	—Our football team didn't win. Tom hurt his leg. —If he hadn't hurt his leg, they might have won.

Circle the correct modal in each sentence.

Example: The doctor ((might)/ might have) help you if you are sick.

1. If you sneeze a lot, you (should / might) have a cold.

2. If you are sick, you (might / should) rest.

3. If hot tea doesn't help, you (could / couldn't) try chicken soup.

4. If you knew the water wasn't clean, you (shouldn't have / shouldn't) drunk it.

5. You (could / couldn't have) understood the lesson very well if you made a C on the test.

6. If you are still sick after three days, you (should / shouldn't) see a doctor.

7. She (could / couldn't have) seen you play if she wasn't at the game!

8. If you don't feel well, you (should / could) get more rest.

9. Rob (should have / could have) won the race if he had tried harder.

Name _____ Date _____

● Writing Assignment
Persuasive Essay

Use with student book page 385.

A.   Build on this word web to brainstorm simple ways to become a leader.

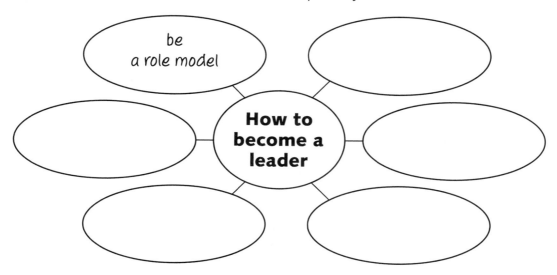

B.   Choose one of your ideas from the mind map above. Think about how you might persuade someone to follow this idea. Do you know of anyone who takes on that leadership role? How and why?

Leadership Role _____	Person _____
How and why people are making this change / taking on this role:	How this person has demonstrated leadership:
_____	_____
_____	_____
_____	_____
_____	_____
_____	_____
_____	_____
_____	_____
_____	_____

Name _____ Date _____

● Writing Assignment
Writing Support

Use with student book page 385.

Spelling: Spelling Rules and Frequently Misspelled Words

English has many spellings rules, and some of them are hard to remember. Here are just a few of those rules.

- **i** before **e,** except after **c** or when it sounds like an **a**
  ceiling, neighbor, receive
- Change **y** to **i** before adding **-es.**
  candy ⟶ candies; sky ⟶ skies; penny ⟶ pennies
- Double the final consonant in many words before adding **-ing** or **-er.**
  pin ⟶ pinning; bat ⟶ batting; skim ⟶ skimming

These words are commonly misspelled:

argument	conscience	grateful	misspell	noticeable
possession	privilege	separate	vacuum	Wednesday

Underline the misspelled words. Rewrite them, fixing the spelling errors.

Example: My grandmother did not take a lot of <u>posessions</u> to the U.S.

My grandmother did not take a lot of possessions to the U.S.

1. I'm very greatful for the priviledge of recieving this gift.

   _____

2. He always seems to mispell "Wenseday."

   _____

3. Mariel is a professional swimer.

   _____

4. Mr. and Mrs. Olafssen had an arguement about geting a new vaccuum cleaner.

   _____

5. Isabel is always runing off to partys!

   _____

6. Your wieght gain is barely noticable; I did not even percieve it!

   _____

7. I can't beleive that they stoped giving out peanuts on airplanes!

   _____

8. I cannot in good concience seperate these puppyies from thier mother.

   _____

Name _____ Date _____

● Writing Assignment
Revising

Use with student book page 385.

- In order to persuade people, you need to use persuasive language. Tell people about the positive results they will have if they follow your suggestion. Give advice about what to do. Here are some examples of persuasive language:

If you want to...	You should...	It is a good idea to...

- Give reasons and examples with your statements. Refer to facts, actual events, your experiences, and other people's experiences. Giving examples helps to convince your reader that your advice is good because it has worked for other people.

Read the following sentences. Revise them to include persuasive language and a concrete example.

Example: To be safe, wear a helmet.	If you want to be safe, you should wear a helmet. The doctor told me if I hadn't been wearing a helmet in my biking accident last summer, I might have been seriously hurt.
1. Do you want to meet new friends? Join an after-school club.	
2. Listen and sing along to music to improve your pronunciation.	
3. Keep your room clean.	
4. Eat fruits and vegetables.	

Name _____ Date _____

● Writing Assignment

Use with student book page 385.

Editing

Mark the mistakes in the following paragraph using the editing marks on page 455 of your student book. Then rewrite the paragraph correctly. Look for errors in spelling, capitalization, punctuation, and grammar.

   If you wanted to develop leadership skills you should start your own club. It don't have to be anything very fancy or formal It could be something simple, like the Sci-Fi Book Club, or the After-School Basketball Group. Just ask some of your freinds to get together once a week and have a discustion about a book you all read, or play a few rounds of basketball. I started an art club like this last year. We got together every wendsday after school and worked on illustrateions. As leader, I was in charge of runing the meetings, stoping argumints, and asking the art teacher for the privelige of using the art room. If I haven't started this group I might not have met my new friend Rachel, and I wouldn't have developed such noticible leadership qualitys. In short, if you will start a group like I did, you have fun and you willn't ever be bored!

_____

_____

_____

_____

_____

_____

_____

_____

_____

_____

_____

_____

Name _____ Date _____

● Vocabulary From the Reading

Use with student book page 390.

> **Key Vocabulary**
> achievement   prestige
> assembly   tournament
> curriculum

A.   Match each Key Vocabulary word to its definition.

Example: __*e*__ assembly

1. _____ tournament

2. _____ curriculum

3. _____ achievement

4. _____ prestige

a. accomplishment

b. long competition consisting of a series of contests

c. respect; honor

d. material taught in school

e. ~~gathering, meeting~~

B.   Circle the correct Key Vocabulary word in each sentence.

Example: Harvard and MIT are schools with a lot of ((prestige) / assembly).

1. The students went to an (achievement / assembly) in the auditorium.

2. Elsa will compete in the gymnastics (tournament / achievement).

3. Which (achievements / prestige) are you most proud of?

4. The (prestige / curriculum) at this school is extremely difficult.

5. He took the job for the (curriculum / prestige), not the money.

C.   Write sentences about your school. Use a Key Vocabulary word in each one.

Example: Last week our school hosted a spelling bee tournament.

1. _____

2. _____

3. _____

Name _____ Date _____

● **Reading Strategy**   *Use with student book page 391.*
   Distinguish Fact from Opinion

> A **fact** is information that is true and that can be proven. An **opinion** is a person's feelings or beliefs about something. Facts can be proven, and opinions cannot be proven. To **distinguish a fact from an opinion**, look for factual proof or clue words that indicate opinions.

Academic Vocabulary for the Reading Strategy		
Word	**Explanation**	
distinguish	to see or understand differences	
locate	to find	

As you read the paragraph, locate statements of fact and opinion. When you finish reading, complete the chart below to help you label facts and opinions.

   The Lord of the Rings is the most important work of fantasy fiction of the twentieth century. It was written by J.R.R. Tolkien and was published in three volumes between 1954 and 1955. There have been stories, novels, songs, movies, and video games based on it. The best movies were made by Peter Jackson between 2001 and 2003. They were not as good as the books, but they were beautifully made and very entertaining.

	Fact	**Proof**
Example:	The Lord of the Rings was written by J.R.R. Tolkien	This information can be researched at a library or Web site

Facts	Proof		Opinions	Clues
1.			1.	
2.			2.	
3.			3.	

Name _____ Date _____

● Text Genre

Use with student book page 392.

Informational Text: Brochure and Newspaper Article

Brochures and Newspaper Articles	
facts and opinions	facts, such as dates, events, names, and services, can be proven; opinions cannot be proven
current events	actual activities happening in the present time
interviews	meetings where information is gathered from someone

A. Read the newspaper article. Write **T** for **true** or **F** for **false**.

Woman Finds Snake in Tub

Appleton, WI—46-year old apartment resident Regina Bailey was shocked yesterday morning when she found a ten-foot snake in her bathtub. Police are investigating, but they suspect that the snake is an escaped pet. Ms. Bailey told the *Chronicle,* "I think it's crazy that people are allowed to have snakes as pets."

Example: __T__ A news item is an example of a current event.

1. _____ The newspaper interviewed the woman who found the snake.

2. _____ Ms. Bailey tells the *Chronicle* a fact.

3. _____ The name of the town and the name of the woman are examples of facts.

4. _____ It is an opinion that the woman found a snake in her tub.

B. Read the brochure. Then write **T** for **true** and **F** for **false** next to each statement.

Camp Wampanoag: The Best Summer Your Kid Will Ever Have!

Founded in 1970, Camp Wampanoag offers two-month camp programs for youths from ages 8 to 18. Here's what some campers have to say about us:

• *Wampanoag is the most fun I ever had. Mom, if you're reading this, <u>please send me back!</u>* —Flavio Montes, age 13

• *Wampanoag is the best!* —Aisha Jones, age 12

1. _____ The heading at the top of the brochure states a fact.

2. _____ The first sentence of the brochure states a fact.

3. _____ The brochure contains the opinions of two kids who went to the camp.

Name _____ Date _____

● Reading Comprehension

Use with student book page 401.

Academic Vocabulary for the Reading Comprehension Questions	
Word	Explanation
factor	someone or something that actively contributes toward a result
resource	a supply of support, money, knowledge, or anything needed

A. Summarize the readings. Summarize the information in the brochure "Science Olympiad."

_____

_____

_____

_____

_____

B. Write your response. What factors might affect a student's decision to enter the Science Olympiad? What resources do they have to help them participate?

_____

_____

_____

_____

_____

C. Assess the reading strategy. How did distinguishing facts from opinions help you understand the brochure and the article?

_____

_____

_____

_____

_____

Name _____ Date _____

● Text Elements

Purpose and Audience

Use with student book page 401.

> Every piece of writing should have a purpose and an audience. The purpose is the goal the author has for writing. Some purposes, or goals, are to entertain, to inform, to describe, or to persuade. The audience is the group of readers the author is writing for. Authors know whether their readers are young, old, new to the book's subject matter, or experts on the topic. Knowing the purpose and audience helps a writer determine what he writes about, or the focus, and how he writes it.

A. Describe the audience, purpose, and focus of each of the following passages.

1. An apple a day keeps the doctor away,
    But how can the other fruits help?
    Mangoes and pears, why, they scare away bears,
    And peaches make crocodiles yelp!

2. Dessert does not have to be unhealthy; fruit makes an excellent after-meal treat. It's low in calories, high in fiber, and very healthy. If fruit alone doesn't appeal to you, try cooking pears in water with sugar and cinnamon and serve with vanilla yogurt. Or, make a salad of fresh fruits, add honey, and top with cream. Another delicious option is to peel some apples, sprinkle with brown sugar and cinnamon, and bake until they are soft and golden brown.

	Purpose	Audience	Focus
Passage 1			
Passage 2			

B. Go back and look at the two readings from Chapter 1. What is the audience, purpose, and focus of each one?

Title	Purpose	Audience	Focus
Iqbal			
"The Equal Rights Struggle Expands"			

Name _____ Date _____

● Vocabulary From the Reading

Use with student book page 402.

> **Key Vocabulary**
>
> discouraged   pursue
> disheveled   shelter
> incentive

A. Write the Key Vocabulary word for each definition.

Example: _____*disheveled*_____ in a state of disarray; messed up

Word	Definition
1. _____	to chase
2. _____	dissuaded, persuaded against; lost confidence
3. _____	protection; place to find protection
4. _____	motivation

B. Complete each sentence with the correct form of a Key Vocabulary word.

Example: The heavy snow _____*discouraged*_____ us from driving to the store.

1. The police _____ the suspect before they caught him.

2. When Crista woke up and came into the kitchen, her eyes were half-closed,

   and her hair was _____.

3. The prize was my _____ to enter the Science Olympiad.

4. We went hiking and slept in a small _____ in the mountains.

C. Answer the following questions using the Key Vocabulary words.

1. How would you feel if you received a low grade after studying hard for an
   exam?

   _____

2. How would your clothes look after you fell off your bike in a rainstorm?

   _____

3. How do animals such as lions and sharks get their food?

   _____

Name _____ Date _____

● Reading Strategy

Use with student book page 403.

Recognize Imagery

> **Recognizing imagery** helps readers form mental pictures. Imagery helps you to imagine the story using the basic senses: sight, sound, touch, smell, and taste.

In each of the following passages, underline specific words or phrases that evoke images in your mind. Then label them according to which sense they stimulate: **sight, sound, touch, smell,** or **taste.**

Example: _____*smell*_____ Before we even arrived at the front door, we could tell that Mother had an apple pie baking in the oven.

1. _____ The baby chicks were warm, soft, fluffy balls of down.

2. _____ Mrs. Kourian's dress and lipstick were of such a bright shade that it was painful to look at her, even with sunglasses on.

3. _____ The cold night air stung my cheeks and transformed my fingers into icicles.

4. _____ It was pitch dark that night; the only light came from the distant moon and the dim stars behind a thin, hazy fog.

5. _____ Suddenly a crack of thunder pierced the air, and the dog flew for shelter under the table, whimpering and whining with fear.

6. _____ I took a spoonful of Kathy's homemade soup, but it was so salty I almost spat it out!

7. _____ We all slurped the soup quickly and dropped our spoons with a clang into the empty bowls.

8. _____ The sweet, juicy pear was a relief after the spicy chili.

9. _____ The rain pattered loudly against the window all night long.

10. _____ Grandma's spicy sauce jolted my nostrils to attention.

Name _____ Date _____

● Text Genre

Use with student book page 403.

Historical Novel

Historical novels are works of fiction that are set in a specific time period in the past. They contain details that reflect that time period. For example, the way people dressed, spoke, traveled, and ate would be researched by the author and included in the novel. Historical novels have the features below.

Historical Novel	
plot	the action of story
historical setting	where and when a story takes place.
historical details	every aspect of life in another time period, such as the way people lived, how they behaved, and what they wore

A. Write **T** for **true** statements and **F** for **false** statements.

Example: __T__ "A soldier goes to war, becomes wounded, and falls in love with a nurse who is on the enemy's side" is an example of plot.

1. _____ "In ancient Greece, people ate olives, grapes and figs; they also ate lots of fish because they lived by the sea" is an example of historical details.

2. _____ "New England in 1700" is an example of plot.

3. _____ "A story about slavery told from the perspective of a man who was captured in Africa" is an example of a historical novel.

4. _____ "The year 2070 on the planet Venus" is an example of a historical setting.

5. _____ "Yucatán, Mexico, in 1100 A.D." is an example of a historical setting.

B. Complete each sentence with a term from the chart at the top of the page.

Example: The _____plot_____ got interesting when the prince fell in love with an ordinary woman.

1. An interesting _____ I learned from *Iqbal* was that some parents have to sell their children into bondage to pay their debts.

2. The _____ for the beginning of Amin Maalouf's novel *Leo Africanus* is Spain at the end of the fifteenth century.

3. I read a historical novel that contained many _____ about the homes and clothing of the Aztecs.

Name _____ Date _____

● Reading Comprehension

Use with student book page 409.

A. **Retell the story.** Summarize the story "Harriet Tubman: Guide to Freedom."

_____

_____

_____

_____

B. **Write your response.** How would you describe Harriet Tubman? What personal and physical characteristics did she have? How do you think she might have chosen which slaves she was going to help to escape?

_____

_____

_____

_____

C. **Assess the reading strategy.** How did recognizing imagery help you understand the story?

_____

_____

_____

_____

Name _____ Date _____

● Spelling

Use with student book page 409.

Compound Words

Many words are formed by combining two words together. The new word is called a compound word. There is no space between the two words that form the compound word.

Word 1	Word 2	Compound Word
rail	road	railroad
bull	frog	bullfrog
some	day	someday
over	seer	overseer

A. Write the compound word that fits each definition. Hint: The definitions contain the component words.

Example: A word needed to pass forward: a _____password_____

1. A house on a farm: a _____

2. A paper containing news: a _____

3. A person who has run away: a _____

4. A print left by a foot: a _____

B. Write a definition for each compound word. Hint: Break the word down into its two component words.

Example: doorway (noun): _a passage, or way, through a door_

1. cheerleader (noun): _____

2. classroom (noun): _____

3. lamplit (adjective): _____

4. underground (adjective): _____

5. springboard (noun): _____

Name _____ Date _____

● Writing Conventions
Punctuation: Titles of Works

Use with student book page 409.

When you cite, or refer to, the title of a reading, you should:
- <u>Underline</u> or *italicize* the titles of books, newspapers, magazines, and plays.
- Put in "quotation marks" the titles of short stories, articles, chapters, and essays.
- Capitalize the first word and all important words (nouns, pronouns, verbs, adjectives, adverbs, and subordinating conjunctions such as **if, as, that**). Do not capitalize **a, an,** or **the,** conjunctions such **as, and,** or **but,** or prepositions, unless they are the first word in the title. **Note:** In some poems and newspaper articles, only the first word is capitalized. Do not capitalize **the** at the beginning of a newspaper title.
- Use a colon between a title and a subtitle. Capitalize the first letter after the colon.
- Use a comma between the title and author.

We read *Harriet Tubman: Guide to Freedom,* by Ann Petry. We also read "The Equal Rights Struggle Expands." We subscribe to the *Washington Post.*

Fix the punctuation and capitalization in the following sentences.

Example: I enjoyed the book fierce pajamas, An anthology of humor writing.

I enjoyed the book <u>Fierce Pajamas: An Anthology of Humor Writing</u>.

1. Did you read the article <u>study shows why the flu likes the winter</u> in The New York times?

_____

_____

2. The story the Pit And The Pendulum appears in the book The tales of Edgar allan Poe.

_____

_____

3. Was there an article called dinosaurs! in last month's "national geographic" magazine?

_____

_____

4. In class, we read the odyssey by a Greek named Homer.

_____

Name _____   Date _____

● Vocabulary Development
Use with student book page 411.
Spelling of Derivatives

Many English words derive, or come, from other words. These words are called derivatives. It is important to spell the new word correctly. Many times you will need to delete one or more letters from the original word.

A. Add the prefix or suffix indicated to each of the words below to form a new derivative. When you finish, check your work in a dictionary.

Example: judge + -ment (the act or result of judging) _____judgment_____

1. technique + -cal (relating to technique) _____

2. announce + -ment (something announced) _____

3. prestige + -ous (relating to or having prestige) _____

4. irritate + -able (easily irritated) _____

5. probable + -ity (the state of being probable) _____

6. possible + -ity (the state of being possible) _____

7. im- + possible (not possible) _____

8. success + -ful (full of or having success) _____

9. capable + -ity (the state of being capable) _____

10. encourage + -ment (something encouraged) _____

B. Use four of the words you formed in Exercise A in sentences.

1. _____

2. _____

3. _____

4. _____

Name _____ Date _____

● Grammar

Use with student book page 412.

Avoiding Subject and Verb Shifts in Writing

Use a consistent subject and verb tense within a single sentence. If the subject or tense changes, the meaning of the sentence will change.

- Avoid shifts in subject by using one subject in the same way throughout a sentence. Check pronouns against the subject introduced earlier in the sentence.

  The **passengers** should sit so **they** do not fall while the bus is in motion.

- Avoid shifts in verb tense by being consistent with the tense you are writing in.

  The girls **laughed** out loud, and then they **walked** away.

A. Find the error in each sentence. Mark it with editing marks and say whether the shift is in the **subject** or the **verb.**

Example: ____verb____ I opened the book and I ~~see~~ ^saw^ the photo.

1. _____ Sam and Monique entered the Science Olympiad, and she did very well.

2. _____ We watched a documentary about the Underground Railroad, and we had learned a lot.

3. _____ I played in a tennis tournament, and he was really difficult.

4. _____ Last year my brother acted in the school play, but I won't go to see it.

B. Rewrite each sentence, fixing the shifts in subject or verb tense.

Example: Ms. Garcia told us he goes to a baseball game last weekend.
     Ms. Garcia told us she went to a baseball game last weekend.

1. The slaves escaped and start a new life in the North.

   _____

2. We spent the whole year training before we enter the Science Olympiad.

   _____

3. Our team won many competitions, but they did not win the tournament.

   _____

Name _____   Date _____

● Grammar Expansion
Reported Speech (Direct and Indirect Quotes)

When you report a direct quote, you use the exact words that somebody says or said:

> My grandmother always says, "I can't hear anything you say!"
> Jenna said, "I am very tired."

When you report an indirect quote, you need to change the subject to match the speaker and verb tense to match when the person says or said the words. You often insert the word **that** before the indirect quote:

> My grandmother always says that **she can't** hear anything we say.
> Jenna said that **she was** tired.

A.   Change the following direct quotes to indirect quotes.

Example: Bridget said, "I need help."

Bridget said that she needed help. _____

1. Tanja always says, "I am the fastest runner on the team."

    _____

2. Ali told me, "I speak Farsi."

    _____

3. Sean and Alan said, "We are from Ireland."

    _____

4. Mr. Diop tells me, "I have a beautiful house in Dakar."

    _____

B.   Report two things that someone you know always says to you. Report two things that your friends told you recently. Use indirect quotes.

1. _____

2. _____

3. _____

4. _____

Milestones C • Copyright © Heinle

Name _____ Date _____

● Grammar

Use with student book page 413.

Active Voice and Passive Voice

In the active voice, a sentence shows an action performed by a subject.

The **wind** *pushed* the little boat.

The **dog** *chased* the squirrel away.

In the passive voice, the subject receives the action of the verb. Passive voice uses a form of the verb **be** (*is, am are, was, were*), and the subject is moved toward the end of the sentence. Use the passive voice when the action is more important than who or what is doing the action.

The little **boat** was *pushed* by the wind.

The **squirrel** was *chased* by the dog.

A. The subject of the following sentences is either general or unknown. Change the sentences from the active to the passive voice. Concentrate on the underlined parts.

Example: They finally sold the house last week

The house was finally sold last week.

1. Someone renovated the building in 1980.

   _____

2. Someone serves dinner every evening at 6:00 in the main dining room.

   _____

B. The following sentences are awkward. Change them from passive to active voice.

Example: The sandwich was eaten by my sister.

My sister ate the sandwich.

1. A red car is driven by Mr. Abouzaid.

   _____

2. The homework was done by me in one hour.

   _____

3. A poem was read in class by Alice yesterday.

   _____

Name _____   Date _____

● Grammar Expansion
Passive Voice in Different Verb Tenses

You have practiced the active and passive voices in the simple present and simple past. Here is how the passive voice is formed in some other verb tenses:

Tense	Passive Form	Active Form
Present Progressive	The house is being painted.	(Someone) is painting the house.
Future	A new president will be elected.	(The people) will elect a new president.
Present Perfect	Our picnic has been interrupted by a bear.	A bear has interrupted our picnic.
Conditional	You would be eaten by a shark if you swam at that beach!	A shark would eat you if you swam at that beach!

A. Change the sentences from the active to the passive voice. Omit the original subject, which is indefinite.

Example: They will publish his book next spring.

His book will be published next spring.

1. Someone will collect the trash on Friday morning.

   _____

2. People are investigating the crime.

   _____

3. Someone has stolen my wallet!

   _____

B. Change the sentences from the passive to the active voice.

1. The newspaper has been read by everyone in the family.

   _____

2. The project will be completed by all the students.

   _____

3. Your pen will be lost if you don't put it in your pocket.

   _____

● **Writing Assignment**
Research Essay about a Historical Period

Use with student book pages 414–415.

Use this chart to help you organize your thoughts before you write your narrative.

Historical period that interests me:

_____

Titles and authors of source books I will use:

1. _____

2. _____

Aspects of daily life that interest me (examples: food, clothing, work, games):

1. _____ 2. _____ 3. _____ 4. _____

Notes:	Notes:	Notes:	Notes:
_____	_____	_____	_____
_____	_____	_____	_____
_____	_____	_____	_____
_____	_____	_____	_____
_____	_____	_____	_____
_____	_____	_____	_____
_____	_____	_____	_____
_____	_____	_____	_____

Some interesting ideas or direct quotes I want to include:

_____

_____

_____

_____

Name _____ Date _____

● Writing Assignment
Writing Support

Use with student book page 415.

Mechanics: Quotation Marks

Use quotation marks around the exact words or sentences you take from a published source. Always identify where the quotation is from; never copy words or phrases without identifying the source.

- Place periods and commas within the quotation marks at the end of the quotation. Note that a direct quotation begins with a capital letter when it is a full sentence.

- Pieces of sentences can be quoted from sources. Use quotation marks to set them off from your own writing, and use a lowercase letter to begin the quotation.

The following sentences take quotes from "Science Olympiad." Fix any errors in capitalization and punctuation.

Example: The Science Olympiad brochure invites us to imagine "A confetti-filled parade." welcoming us home from the tournament. (Paragraph 3)

The Science Olympiad brochure invites us to imagine "a

confettifilled parade" welcoming us home from the tournament.

1. According to the brochure, the tournament that "Began as a grassroots assembly of science educators" has now become one of the premier science competitions in the nation. (Paragraph 5)

   _____

   _____

2. "The brochure emphasizes that a kid can receive all the benefits and praise that come with being a star athlete," all without throwing, catching, or hitting a ball. (Paragraph 6)

   _____

   _____

3. According to the brochure, "one of Science Olympiad's most important goals is to bring academic competition to the same level of recognition and praise normally reserved for athletic competitors in this country". (Paragraph 6)

   _____

   _____

Name _____ Date _____

● Writing Assignment
Revising Activity

Use with student book page 415.

Read each revision tip. Then rewrite the sentences to make them better.

Revision Tip # 1: Try to use the active voice as much as possible for clearer, more powerful sentences.

First Try	A Better Way to Say It
Example: Greenland was discovered by Vikings in the tenth century.	Vikings discovered and settled Greenland in the tenth century.
1. The pyramids at Chichén-Itzá were built by the Mayans over 1,500 years ago.	
2. Dogs were owned by many people in ancient Rome.	
3. Heavy armor used to be worn to battle by knights in medieval Europe.	

Revision Tip # 2: Always give credit to the source of an idea.

First Try (underlined parts indicate exact words taken from a source text)	A Better Way to Say It
Example: Dolores Huerta thought she could do more by organizing farm workers than by trying to teach their hungry children.	Dolores Huerta felt that she could help the Mexican-American community more by leading a labor movement than by teaching farm workers' children, who were often too hungry to learn.
1. Fulfilling a desire to bring excitement to science competitions, Science Olympiad was founded in 1983 by educators Dr. Gerard J. Putz and John C. Cairns.	
2. The civil rights movement sent shock waves through American society. Many people reconsidered issues of equality and discrimination and became politically involved in their communities. The civil rights movement encouraged other minorities in their fight for equal rights.	

Name _____ Date _____

● Writing Assignment

Use with student book page 416.

Editing Activity

Read the paragraph and find the mistakes. Mark the mistakes in the following paragraph using the editing marks on page 455 of your student book. Then rewrite the paragraph correctly. Pay attention to spelling, capitalization, punctuation, grammar, and word usage.

    For hundreds of years, the Vikings were fear throughout Europe. They were known for burning villages, steal treasures, and taking prisonners. But we were also adventurers who explore the northern seas, settle the icy island of Greenland, and travel as far as Canada. the book the Far Traveler; voyages of a Viking woman by Nancy Marie Brown describes the life and travels of a tenth-century Viking woman named Gudrid. Gudrid "Knew the killing force of the sea, of weeks at the mercy of the winds, of fog that froze on the sails and rigging, when . . . no land, no shelter, was in sight'. Sailing on the high seas was dangerous, but the Vikings have excellent ships. Nancy Marie Brown wrote that the first time I saw a Viking ship in the water I wanted to sail away on it.

_____

_____

_____

_____

_____

_____

_____

_____

_____

_____

_____

_____

_____